491-6609046 ait
491-668
AlT

A GEOGR

A GEOGRAPHY OF THE WELSH LANGUAGE 1961–1991

John Aitchison

and

Harold Carter

CARDIFF
UNIVERSITY OF WALES PRESS
1994

British Library Cataloguing-in-Publication Data

A catalogue record for this book is available from the British Library

ISBN   0-7083-1236-5

Cover design by Design Principle, Cardiff
Typeset at the University of Wales Press
Printed at The Alden Press, Oxford

This book is dedicated to the staff and students of the Department of Geography, University of Wales, Aberystwyth, 1917–1992

Contents

Preface

This book seeks to describe and explain the changing geography of the Welsh language, with particular reference to the period 1961–91. It updates, expands and re-evaluates findings contained in our earlier volume *The Welsh Language 1961–1981: An Interpretative Atlas* (University of Wales Press, 1983). That publication was dedicated to the life and work of the late Emrys Bowen, Gregynog Professor of Geography, at the University College of Wales, Aberystwyth (1929–68); the dedication that fronts this particular text is much less personal, and draws attention to the fact that in 1992 the Department of Geography, as it then was, reached its seventy-fifth anniversary.

It is a matter of great pride to the authors, both of whom have held the Gregynog Chair of Human Geography, that over the seventy-five years of its existence, the department identified as one of its main tasks the interpretation of the human and cultural landscape of Wales. That commitment was established by H. J. Fleure and was continued by his successors and their colleagues. It was in due course totally proper that the department appointed G. J. Jones to develop courses which could be taken through the medium of Welsh, and that the first Dean of the Faculty of Welsh Medium Studies should have been a Gregynog Professor of Geography.

Within the broader field of human geographical studies the changing spatial distribution of the Welsh language was very much a central concern of the department. D. Trevor Williams pioneered the detailed mapping of census data and his work was elaborated upon in relation to successive censuses by J. Gareth Thomas, Emrys Jones and E. G. Bowen. Equally influential has been the work of W. T. R. Pryce on the historical geography of the language. More recent studies by John Giggs (a former postgraduate of the department) on social and class linkages has given extra depth to the appreciation of language patterns in Wales. Glyn Williams, who was an undergraduate and postgraduate student of the department, has also produced important work in relation to class structure, and in addition has written cogently on socio-linguistics. Over the years numerous language-focused theses have been undertaken by both undergraduates and postgraduates of the department.

Interest in the language has not solely been limited to its spatial expression. The major tradition of community studies which so characterized the department during the 1940s was initiated by Alwyn D. Rees, one of the great defenders of the language. This tradition was primarily devoted to communities as such, but they were usually communities where the Welsh language was a crucial attribute. The work of David Jenkins, Tom Jones Hughes, Trefor M. Owen and again Emrys Jones is of classic significance. Over more recent times the commitment of Aberystwyth geographers to community interests has been maintained and extended with the formative involvement of the Rural Surveys Research Unit (directed by Professor John Aitchison and Dr Bill Edwards) in the Welsh Jigso initiative. This initiative, which is currently coordinated by former students of the department – Dr Liz Hughes and Claire Goold – seeks to encourage rural and urban communities throughout Wales to undertake detailed appraisals of local needs and aspirations, with a view to formulating action and development plans. This applied, advocacy approach adds a highly distinctive dimension to the long tradition of community studies at Aberystwyth. In this context, it is also not without relevance that a magnificent bequest, which has helped to provide the University of Wales Centre for Advanced Welsh and Celtic Studies with its new building adjacent to the National Library at Aberystwyth, was made by Elwyn Davies who had himself been a product and part of the Aberystwyth geographical tradition.

This book is a modest acknowledgement to the work of the many scholars and students who, over seventy-five years and in varying ways, have contributed to the very special image and standing of Geography at Aberystwyth. The tradition that they have helped to create lives on.

JOHN AITCHISON and HAROLD CARTER
University of Wales, Aberystwyth
January, 1994

Acknowledgements

The authors wish to express their gratitude to Philip Jones of the Rural Surveys Research Unit for the compilation of census maps; to Paula Jones of the International Centre for Protected Landscapes (University of Wales, Aberystwyth) for a meticulous editing of the final text; and to Ian Gulley, Mike Gelly Jones, David Griffiths and Geraint Hughes for the preparation of selected diagrams and maps.

Ward data from 1991 census was provided through the Census Dissemination Unit at the University of Manchester, with the support of ESRC/GISC.

CHAPTER 1

Language and Ethnicity

The importance of your learning – and conforming to – the rules spelled out, entry by entry, in *The Official Politically Correct Dictionary and Handbook* cannot be overemphasized. For, as linguists Edward Sapir and Benjamin Wharf suspected as early as the 1940s – and postmodernist theory has confirmed – language is not merely the mirror of society, it is the major force in 'constructing' what we perceive as 'reality'. (Beard and Cerf, 1992, xiii).

Linguistic Relativism

It might seem odd, even perverse, to begin an analysis of the changing geography of the Welsh language with a quotation from *The Official Politically Correct Dictionary and Handbook* (Beard and Cerf, 1992). Its relevance to the present study is that it serves to emphasize the importance that is attached to language, even to the extent of using it to manipulate culture and ideology. Significantly, Beard and Cerf preface their tract with a reference to George Orwell's 1984 – 'It was intended that when Newspeak had been adopted once and for all and Oldspeak forgotten, a heretical thought . . . should be literally unthinkable, at least so far as thought is dependent on words.'

The attempt to impose a politically correct vocabulary, the Sapir–Wharf hypothesis, and George Orwell's Newspeak are all expressions of the same belief – that the languages people speak profoundly shape the way in which they think and act. As Mandelbaum has observed:

Human beings do not live in the objective world alone, nor alone in the world of social activity as ordinarily understood, but are very much at the mercy of the particular language which has become the medium of expression for the society. It is quite an illusion to imagine that one adjusts to reality essentially without the use of language and language is merely an incidental means of solving problems of communication and reflection. (Mandelbaum, 1949, 162)

Needless to say, such a relativistic stance, which can also be seen as 'a reaction against the nominalist position originating in Platonic and Aristotlian [*sic*] philosophy and popular throughout the nineteenth century, that knowledge of reality is not affected by language'

(Steinfatt, 1989), is not universally accepted. It would seem, for instance, to be at odds with Chomsky's proposal of 'an innate schema of grammar in humans as a necessary postulate to account for language acquisition in children' (Steinfatt, 1989, 39). Be this as it may, linguistic relativism, developed in the 1940s and current since, is in keeping with post-modernism. Post-modernism is obsessed with deconstruction, iconography and semiotics. These are concerned respectively with the significance of language, visual images, and signs and symbols – all modes of perception and expression of the environment in which people live and have their being. Likewise, all are deeply ritualized and conditioned by language. To quote from an interpretation of the cultural anthropology of Mary Douglas,

> Ritual carries or transmits collective information, like language. But it is also true that language acts like a ritual, and its structures – its codes – are part of society's arsenal of ritual utilized in the periodic affirmation of social order. To speak is to perform a ritual, and partake, intentionally or not, in the affirmation and reproduction of basic social relations and commonly held values. (Wuthnow, 1984, 104)

Bringing these rather abstruse academic ideas down to the clichés of everyday life, it is often observed when no common ground can be found between two people 'that they are not speaking the same language'; that a meeting of minds is impossible because views are totally incompatible and that the basis lies in the lack of a common language which is the necessary criterion for a common understanding.

At this point it is appropriate to allude to the important linkage between language and ethnicity, and in particular Welsh ethnic identity. Seeking to define ethnicity, Anthony D. Smith writes that:

> it relates mainly to a sense of community based on history and culture, rather than to any collectivity or to the concept of ideology. In this, I follow the emendation proposed by Epstein to the literature of 'situational' ethnicity in which the growth of a sense of the collective self is treated as an important part of a group (especially ethnic) identity and solidarity. Only here, the sense of self is viewed through the prism of symbols and mythologies of the community's heritage . . . The core of ethnicity, as it has been transmitted in the historical record and as it shapes individual experience, resides in this quartet of 'myths, memories, values and symbols' and in the characteristic forms or styles and genres of certain historical configurations of populations. (Smith A. D., 1986, 14/15)

The conclusion from the above discussion is quite clear; that identity, and especially ethnic identity and the culture on which it is based, are dependent on a communality. That communality is derived from an inheritance which is passed on through language. There is an alternative basis in religion, which also generates a unifying view of the nature of the environment and specifies accepted modes of behaviour and patterns of living. It, too, has played its part in Welsh ethnic identity, but the manifest implication of the debate thus far

2

is that to be Welsh, in any meaningful way, a person must speak, or at least understand, Welsh. Otherwise he or she is no more than someone dwelling in a defined area called Wales; and ethnically no more than a version of provincial English, or more tactfully someone who can be called British, like the Geordies or the Cornish, Cumbrians or perhaps even Liverpudlians – all variations on a central theme. To broach these matters is inevitably to enter a field of major controversy. Responses to such assertions are always immediate and angry, for to deny Welshness to non-Welsh-speakers whose families have lived in Wales from time immemorial is to touch a very raw nerve. Moreover, it is possible to cite Celtic countries where language is now of peripheral significance in the definition of identity. The Irish language by now is only a relict feature of being Irish (Hindley, 1992), although it is possible to argue that Lallans is an indicator of being Scottish, much more so than Gaelic. Again, across the Atlantic, American identity is not based on a different language, though the appearance of American English dictionaries might cause some hesitation.

Since it is at least an implicit assumption of this analysis that the Welsh language has a significance over and beyond its role as a means of communication, a role to which at least some would relegate it, it is pertinent briefly to note the assertions and denials of the association of language with ethnic identity. Out of the very many discussions on this topic, it is sufficient to select one which is a good representative, and John Osmond's paper 'The modernisation of Wales' (1989) is as good as any. Moreover, it appeared in a volume appropriately entitled *National Identity in the British Isles* (Evans, 1989). The only reservation to be made at this point is that we are not concerned here with the issue of nationalism, that is whether ethnic identity should be associated with political autonomy (Dofny and Akiwowo, 1980; Smith, 1986; Williams, C. H., 1982, 1991). That is a separate matter, although one which it is difficult to elide.

Osmond's paper develops a critique by Ned Thomas (1988) of the attitudes of Dafydd Elis Thomas (1988), the then President of Plaid Cymru. It is worth a lengthy quotation –

> Part of the focus of the attack was Elis Thomas's *Western Mail* article about Wales's image . . . The argument was over the vexed issue of in-migration and the response to it that is both possible and appropriate. The thrust of Ned Thomas's attack was that Plaid Cymru's leader was seeking a Wales, or perhaps recognising the inevitability of a future Wales where the Welsh speaking community would not be the defining essence of Welsh identity and nationhood, but part of the nation, 'a kind of ethnic substratum'.

Osmond proceeds to quote Ned Thomas as maintaining that there can be no sense of territorial belonging in Wales without the language, and then to provide his own answer.

> But Ned Thomas ignores a number of powerful elements which guide the sensibility of the English-speaking Welsh: primarily a sense of responsibility for their communities, but beyond that other factors like identification with a landscape and a growing structure of institutions that above else . . . define the territory of Wales. (Osmond, 1989, 88)

3

Another contribution to this debate is that by Giggs and Pattie (1991; 1992 a and b). In an analysis of census data they explore statistical relationships between language, social class and birthplace. Among other revelations, they demonstrate that:

> Welsh-speakers collectively were an important component of the élite service class chiefly in metropolitan south Wales and its industrial hinterland and secondarily in north-east Wales. In contrast, in the Welsh-speaking rural heartland of Wales (i.e. Gwynedd, Dyfed and Powys), Welsh-speakers were actually under-represented in the service class. (Giggs and Pattie, 1991, 27)

It follows from this, and the associated analysis, that contemporary Welsh society is plural rather than homogeneous, divided rather than cohesive. . . 'There are in Welsh society profound internal divisions based on ethnicity, language (with all its attendant cultural manifestations) and class' (p.28).

It is certainly possible that some of these conclusions are no more than the product of statistical analysis at a very crude aggregate scale and would need to be supported by studies at a behavioural level. But the general summary is in line with Osmond's presentation.

> There seems to be evidence of a disquieting preoccupation with cultural élitism among some Welsh-speaking Welsh people. It is heartening that proficiency in Britain's oldest language (hitherto long derided) now provides dignity, social prestige and opportunity in Wales. At the same time it is profoundly disheartening that a few zealots can seriously assert that the English-speaking majority, who constitute 77.6 per cent of the Welsh-born residents in 1981 . . . are 'not *really* Welsh'. Moreover, the problems are not simply those of proficiency in the Welsh language being touted as the essential qualification for Welsh nationality, rather than mere nativity, which is deemed a qualification in the majority of countries: there are attendant cultural, political and economic implications. (Giggs and Pattie, 1991, 29)

The authors go on to quote a letter by Alan Watkins to the *Observer* of 19 February 1989:

> Thus the Welsh establishment is still Welsh-speaking, literary but philistine, Nonconformist (with a bias towards Calvinism), hostile towards Labour and, above all, essentially pacifist. So it is that Welsh school children are asked to admire the works of second rate versifiers while remaining ignorant of the fact that, in the Great War, Wales proportionately sacrificed more men than any other part of the UK. Likewise, children will be told of the exploits, largely made up, of Owain Glyndŵr but not about the very real achievements of the South Wales Borderers and the Welsh regiment. (Giggs and Pattie, 1991, 29–30)

A polemic is necessarily unbalanced, but an appeal to the teaching of imperial history is perhaps the most unlikely part of the letter.

Here, then, is the nub of the debate over the role of language: one which has no easy resolution. At this point, too, as was noted earlier, and as Osmond's and Giggs and Pattie's comments imply, the issues of nationalism as well as ethnic identity enter. On the one hand there is the contention that Welsh identity can rest only on the language, for there is nothing else; all other aspects of separateness having been lost. Thus, there is no distinctive Welsh legal system for the English system was imposed at the time of the Union. But, it could be argued that political separation is a necessary condition for the survival of the language. Against that is set the view that with an enhanced institutional base, both political and economic, a distinctive Wales can be created in which the language would be incidental. It would be a Wales necessarily independent for only under that condition could the essential institutional framework be effectively developed. The USA and Ireland now, apart from its Catholicism, are identified not by language, or indeed by culture, but by the political, social and economic structures which make them different.

This is the view expressed in typical fashion by Gwyn A. Williams. 'Wales is an artefact which the Welsh produce; the Welsh make and remake Wales day by day and year after year . . . It is not history which does this; it is not traditions which do this' (Williams, G. A., 1979, 23). Thus he rejects the role of culture, defined as inherited ideas and traditions and their attached values, in this remaking process, and presumably, if it is what those resident in Wales want as they remake Wales, the language too. Being Welsh, for example, would be possible without having read a single line of the language's literature, even of second-rate versifiers, and being totally ignorant of its traditions for they would be something to make anew. The country's history would be an irrelevance. It is difficult to envisage under such conditions what being Welsh would mean, other than having a government more to the left, and that with no guarantee of permanency, and shouting for the rugby team on international days! But whatever the consequent state, such an ideal is in contrast to that of the language protagonists; it condemns 'a fossilized liberal nonconformist Welsh nationalism with its fixed concept of Welsh identity' and 'the tunnel vision within large swathes of the Welsh-speaking intelligentsia' (Williams, E. W., 1989, 58) and deploys a view of a socialist republic on the land of Wales where the language used would be of incidental significance. Perhaps the crux of the problem is that there are two ethnolinguistic groups in Wales, the Welsh and the Anglo-Welsh, but with both attempting to claim some form of priority in representative status.

These sorts of problems have achieved a more immediate relevance and a new turn in the post-modern world. Post-modernism has many definitions, but it is crucially marked by the collapse of ordered certainties and of monolithic structures. Nowhere has that been more apparent than in the field of imperial disintegration and political nationalism. The once 'united' systems are breaking apart into older constituent pieces, which are as much defined by their histories and by their languages and religions as by any other criteria. The past and the cultural inheritance do seem to matter as the imposed rigidities dissolve. Certainly in the Baltic republics, as in the break up of the USSR and Yugoslavia, language and religion seem to have played central roles. Freedom from centralized socialist coercion is demanded so that democratic institutions can ensure the survival of language and culture.

The purpose of this introductory section is not to make any contribution to the substantive debate which it has broached. The burgeoning field of ethnolinguistic identity theory (Gudykunst, 1989) is broad in compass and deals with speech accommodation, language attitudes and second language acquisition. The topic has been raised here simply to underline the significance of the relationship between language and ethnicity. If language is solely a means of communication, an alphabetical as opposed to a numerical system, then its loss would mean little. Indeed, it could be conceived as an advantage, a view certainly held by a number of people in Wales. Its disappearance would eliminate one of those divisive elements in Wales, which Giggs and Pattie identified, in favour of an international language of great richness. But as we have endeavoured to demonstrate, language is much more than a means of communication. Not only does it carry a view of the environment, using that word in its proper inclusive sense, but through its vocabulary and its structure, through the associations generated by its literature, through the symbol which it is and the symbols which it transmits, it creates a distinctive identity which is at once a derivative of tradition and an expression of the present. It is difficult to envisage an ethnic identity as defined earlier without an awareness through the language of the myths, memories, values and symbols of Welshness. Indeed, where identity has to be created so does a language; perhaps modern Hebrew is the best example.

If one believes that the salvation of Wales and its language rests on some form of total revolution of society as it is now constituted, then a mere geographical analysis of the patterns of language change (as presented here) will be considered a waste of time. If, however, one associates language with ethnic identity and looks to change as giving insight into the operative processes within and related to that identity, and it would be equally relevant within an independent democratic Wales, then mapping and the interpretation of associated distributions are central to language issues. What this text is designed to present is a great deal more than the distribution of contrasted sounds and grammars.

Much of the foregoing discussion has entered marginally and tentatively into the field of sociolinguistics, whereas this study is essentially a contribution to a parallel field of geolinguistics. As early as 1965 the American Society of Geolinguistics was formed; and the series *Discussion Papers in Geolinguistics*, edited by Colin Williams, has appeared since 1980. In definition of geolinguistics it is appropriate to quote Williams's words:

> Its specific concern is with the relationship between languages and their physical and human settings. Thus it may seek among other things to illuminate the socio-spatial context of language use and language choice; to measure language distribution and variety; 'to assess the relative practical importance, usefulness and availability' of different languages from the economic, psychological, political and cultural standpoints of specific speech milieux; to understand variations in their basic grammatical, phonological and lexical structure and to measure and 'map their genetic, historical and geographical affiliations and relationships'. (Williams, C. 1984)

The quotations within the above extract are included among the aims of the American Society of Geolinguistics, and are in their turn derived from Mario Pei's book *Invitation to Linguistics* (1971). It is clear that this text can in no way cover the whole field of geolinguistics. It is however firmly set in the speciality of geolinguistics and focuses on the analysis of language patterns, their historical development and contemporary form. Language mapping is more than an academic exercise. It is an enquiry into the identity of a people and how that identity survives in the late twentieth century.

Spatial Dimensions of Ethnicity, Culture and Language

Any discussion of ethnic identity of necessity introduces another dimension – territoriality and the spatial context of that identity. World events in the 1990s have brought that relationship to the forefront of political consideration; the drawing of lines on maps has become crucial. But the relationship of ethnicity to land is a very complex one which in its totality is beyond the scope of this discussion. However, three aspects can be abstracted.

(i) Ethnicity and the nation state

The nation state is a political entity, but one which in modern history has been more and more correlated with ethnic character, so that nation and ethnic group have almost become synonymous (Gellner, 1983). Certainly that was not true of early empires where hegemony was established over a multiplicity of peoples. But it has been the collapse of imperial systems over the last century which has produced, or in part been produced by, a determination among subject peoples to control their own destinies. Interpretation of these processes has produced an immense literature (Dofny and Akiwowo, 1980; Gellner, 1983; Smith A. D., 1986). As far as Wales is concerned the central issue is the relationship of the Welsh language, as the hallmark of Welsh identity, to Welsh nationalism (Williams C. H., 1982; Evans, 1989). This is a matter of widespread concern and is the crux of a major problem for Plaid Cymru. To associate itself too closely with language issues means association with less than 20 per cent of the voters; to distance itself from the language alienates its basic core of support in Welsh-speaking Wales. Although this has been the most intensely discussed of the territorial relationships, it is not one which this analysis seeks to highlight. That said, even describing basic language distributions inevitably brings it to the fore.

(ii) Ethnicity, culture and the culture region

An attempt was made in the previous section to present a brief definition of ethnic identity. The collective tradition there outlined has much in common with the concept of culture, although culture can be taken as a broader, all-embracing term which includes the manifest representations of a way of life, both material and immaterial. Early in the development of anthropology, attempts were made to relate cultures to spatial contexts and the notion of the culture region became an integral part of cultural anthropology, and indeed of human geography. The very use of the word 'region' again introduces as massive a literature as that on the definition of culture. But it is hardly pertinent to develop that theme, rather is it

7

more relevant to consider the idea of the culture region itself. 'The culture-area concept has its origin in the practical exigencies of American ethnographic research, as a heuristic device for mapping and clarifying the tribal groups of North and South America' (Harris, 1968, 374). Its early use was characterized by an emphasis on the linkage with environmental conditions. Perhaps the nearest equivalent in relation to Wales was the late E. G. Bowen's presidential address to the Institution of British Geographers (Bowen, 1959), entitled 'Le Pays de Galles'. Bowen sought to 'study the interrelationships of systematic geographical phenomena in different parts of Wales' and he went on to assert that 'in one area at least, these interrelationships produce a characteristic way of life integrated with the physical setting' (Bowen, 1959, 23). That one area constituted the true 'Pays de Galles', the land of the Welsh-speaking, the area that was later to be called 'Y Fro Cymraeg'. However, few now would attempt to argue for a basis in the physical environment.

At this point two further sets of ideas need to be introduced. The first is Wilbur Zelinsky's 'schematic three-dimensional model of cultural systems' (Zelinsky, 1973a, 1973b), which is shown in Figure 1.1. In it three intrinsic components of cultural regions are identified as mentifacts, sociofacts and artifacts. The breakdown of the mentifact component is detailed as religion, language, the arts, magic, folklore, to which rather diverse list a covering 'etcetera' is added. The other two components are not so detailed. Successive divisions into subcultures is envisaged, based on components such as occupations, presumably a surrogate for economic character, social composition and ideological orientation. It must be admitted that in its detail it is not a particularly convincing schema. But in its general representation it is of real value; for it displays the complexity of components which make up a culture and hence the difficulty of turning them into a cartographic form.

It follows that the second set of ideas is directly related to the mapping of the various components of culture. Three basic approaches can be distinguished. The first is usually referred to as a 'cultural block' procedure. Here, components are treated as being mutually exclusive so that their distribution defines the discrete region. That in reality is a most unlikely situation. A second approach is one which can be referred to as 'radial concentric' in that it views a culture as declining in intensity and integrity from a core to a periphery where it is weaker and mixed with neighbouring cultures. The third approach can be termed 'polythetic' for it is one where all the components are seen as having differing, even dissimilar, distribution patterns, but where an area of maximum overlap can be derived and identified as a culture region of sufficient homogeneity to be meaningful, a climax area.

The block procedure has seldom been used, but the other two have been considerably developed. From the outset the polythetic procedure has been the most frequently employed. It was favoured by the doyen of culture region definition, the anthropologist A. L. Kroeber. His two classic works were, *Handbook of the Indians of California* (1925) and *Cultural and Natural Areas of Native North America* (1939). As Harris writes, 'he approached the construction of cultural areas by means of increasingly elaborate statistical

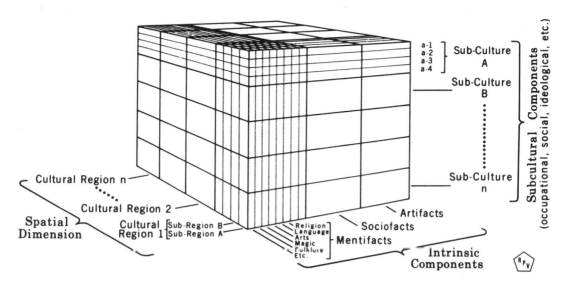

A schematic, three-dimensional representation of cultural systems.

Figure 1.1

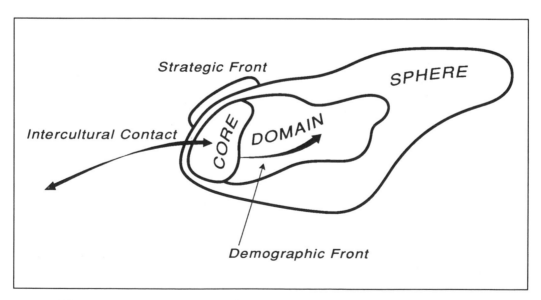

The morphology of a Culture Region (after D. Meinig)

Figure 1.2

manipulation of disjointed trait-element lists consisting of as many as six thousand items' (Harris, 1968, 339). Harris adds that no one has ever taken up his suggestion 'to measure intensity and climax by counting fragmented trait lists' (p.341). Even so, the development of multivariate statistical methods, especially factor and cluster analyses, have enabled procedures in keeping with Kroeber's concept to be carried out. Such studies have tended not to engage in hypothesis-testing or model-building however; they have usually been inductive exercises using as large a number of variables as possible to establish areas of common character. Needless to say, studies of this type do not escape the criticism as to the choice and relative significance of the variables used. Several typological analyses have been carried out for Wales using language, socio-economic and political (voting patterns) data (Carter and Williams, 1978; Williams, C. H., 1982; Carter and Aitchison 1986).

(iii) A model of a culture region

The only attempt to provide a model of a culture region is that proposed by Meinig (1965) in his consideration of the Mormon area of the United States. It is a more specified version of the radial concentric schema and based on one criterion only, in his case membership of the Church of the Latter Day Saints. He contended that it was possible to identify three sections associated with diminishing dominance. The first of them he called the 'core', 'the zone of concentration displaying the greatest density of occupation and intensity of organisation, and the area most representative of the definitive characteristics of the culture'. The second Meinig termed the 'domain', an 'outlying area dominated by the patterns of the culture under study but with less intensity and homogeneity'. There are lower densities and local allegiances. The third part is called the 'sphere' where elements of the culture 'may be apparent but not dominant'. These elements may indeed be in the form of alien influences spreading into local cultures. The model is shown in Figure 1.2 where other features are added. The first is the localization of cultural contact and interaction in terms of a line of 'intercultural contact', which Meinig envisaged as a dominant routeway. The second is a 'strategic front' where the greatest physical threat to a culture is concentrated; 'where that danger is military in type, concentrations of walls and fortresses, garrisons and depots, may be readily apparent; where it is merely political it may be more diffuse and less obvious.' Finally, there is the 'demographic front' where actual population movements involve a physical extension of the core or domain.

It is clear that the model is conceived in terms of an expanding culture region and it is not easily adapted to decline. But the basic ideas are easily identified in the Welsh language context. Thus, for example, the demographic front can in contemporary terms be interpreted as the inflow of non-Welsh-speaking migrants into Wales over the last two decades. In more general terms, the division of Wales, such as that adopted by Rees Pryce, into Welsh-speaking, bilingual and English-speaking zones corresponds to core, domain and sphere (1978a). A major criticism of Meinig's study is that there is no attempt to justify a threefold division. Presumably the implication is that an analysis of relevant data, church membership in his case, would show borders with steeper gradients of change at the boundaries. But no such measures were undertaken and the division into core, domain and sphere is proposed without any attempt at justification. Meinig's work was based simply on church membership but subsequent studies have attempted to add landscape elements (Francaviglia, 1970). The model has been used by Carter (1969; 1976) in his interpretation of the referenda on the Sunday opening of licensed premises in Wales as a criterion of a culture region, and by Pryce in his historical studies of the language. It is a useful heuristic device, and indeed is implicit in most studies of language patterns in Wales; inevitably so perhaps. Thus, E. G. Bowen's inner and outer Wales (1964) are no more than core and sphere, whilst, of course, *Y Fro Gymraeg* is the classic core of a culture region. It is evident that much of the work on Wales has been concerned with only one symbol of culture and that it would be more appropriate to refer to language areas and to keep to the notion of ethnicity as represented by language. There have been few attempts to map other criteria apart from Carter's use of referenda data. But there is no problem in applying Meinig's concept to language alone for, as has been noted, his work was based solely on religion.

Ethnolinguistic Vitality

Having considered the links between language and ethnic identity and the possibility of deriving some model of the ethnic or culture area, it is appropriate to consider the issue of linguistic vitality (Giles, Bourhis and Taylor, 1977); for it is this concept more than any other that guides the present study of language change in Wales.

Figure 1.3 identifies a set of structural variables which determine degrees of linguistic vitality. Three contributory factors are specified. They are status, demography and institutional support. Status is divided into social status – the degree of esteem a linguistic group affords itself – and economic status – the degree of control a language group has gained over the economic life of its nation, region or community. To these are added socio-historical status or the symbolic value of the language, and the evaluation of the language both from within and from without.

The second set of variables is termed demographic and includes two aspects. The first is the relation of language to territory and the numbers and proportions within that territory. Closely related to those features are the standard demographic processes of population change, including increase or decrease by natural causes (the excess or otherwise of births over deaths), and by in- or out-migration. The only unusual element in this schema is that of mixed marriages which have an obvious consequence on language shift (Harrison, 1978). Figure 1.4 seeks to summarize these demographic movements and their impact on numbers of Welsh-speakers in a simple model. In addition to the population variables noted above, it also takes into account second-language learning and language loss (i.e., subsequent rejection of the language by native speakers or learners), both of which to varying degrees affect numbers of speakers within particular localities.

The third set of variables is related to institutional support and stresses a whole gamut of formal and informal sources of language maintenance. These include the role of government, the media, education, religion and a host of others.

11

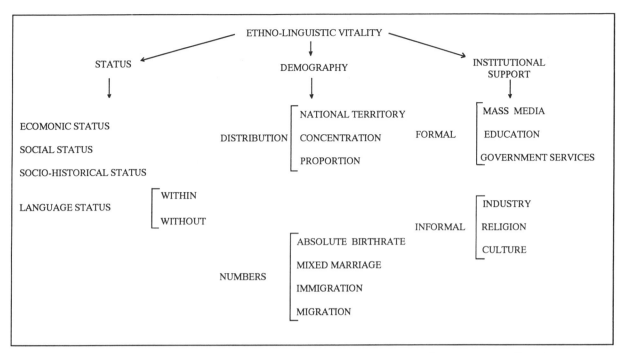

A taxonomy of the structural variables affecting ethno-linguistic vitality (after Giles, Bourhis and Taylor)

Figure 1.3

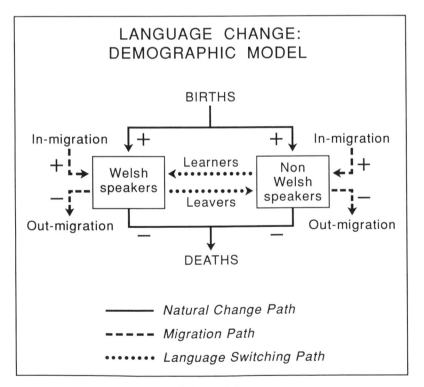

Figure 1.4

Simple identification of such a set of factors in seeking to explain the process of language change has not been without its critics of course, and there are clearly alternative conceptual and theoretical models that could be structured; for example, approaches based on materialism, political economy or critical socio-cultural theory (Jackson, 1989; Williams, G. 1992). It cannot be gainsaid, however, that the variables included have been (and are) of central significance in shaping the development of the Welsh language; accordingly they figure prominently in the historical review and statistical analyses that form the basis of this study. Before moving on to consider such substantive matters, however, it is necessary to draw attention to a number of technical matters associated with language mapping.

CHAPTER 2

Mapping the Welsh Language

Studies of the changing geography of the Welsh language have drawn heavily upon data derived from national population censuses. Other sources of information have been used (e.g., church records, local authority statistics for schools), but it is to successive census enumerations that most researchers of have turned for insights into regional patterns and trends. Unfortunately, the censuses themselves have not assured researchers a consistent set of statistics for purposes of comparative analysis. The questions asked have changed, the population bases have been continually modified, and, most problematic of all, the spatial units (administrative divisions) to which the data relate have varied. Census data need to be treated with care, especially when, as in this study, they are being used to describe patterns and trends over time.

Censuses of the Welsh Language 1891–1981

The first formal census of the Welsh language was undertaken in 1891. The data collected indicated the numbers of persons aged two years old and over who were monoglot Welsh-speakers and those who had a facility in both Welsh and English. However, as Southall (1895) was soon to point out, the enumeration process was defective on several counts and failed to yield a reliable record of the state of the language at the time. The language statistics were treated in cursory fashion by the census authorities and were presented only for registration districts and counties. These divisions were largely unrelated to existing administrative areas and certainly lacked the fine spatial detail necessary for an appreciation of geographical variations. The fact that certain localities along the Welsh border were excluded from the enumeration, while others actually located in England were included, confused the issue even further.

The population census for 1901 again recorded numbers of Welsh-speakers, but this time data related to persons aged three years and over. This particular threshold has been maintained through successive censuses to the present. In terms of the data themselves Welsh-speakers were categorized according their sex and age characteristics. Statistics were collated for administrative counties, county boroughs, municipal boroughs, urban districts and rural districts. These same conditions also applied to the census of 1911, although with more detailed subdivisions according to age. The most significant feature of the 1921 census was that for the first time data were presented for civil parishes, as well as the administrative divisions used in the two previous censuses. Numbers of Welsh-speakers in urban areas with populations over 50,000 were also detailed.

For each of the first four censuses it is worth noting that variable adjustments were made to the total figures to take account of persons who had failed to make language returns. Inevitably, these adjustments, which were largely based on the language of heads of households (where this was known), introduced a degree of uncertainty into the data. The 1931 and 1951 censuses (there was no census in 1941) were broadly similar in format to that adopted in 1921, but with the Welsh-speaking population in smaller urban areas (20,000–50,000) also being specified in published tabulations. In 1961 the spatial frames for the aggregation of statistics on Welsh-speakers included the small areas or enumeration districts used in the initial compilation of returns. This was a significant advance, although few researchers have taken advantage of the opportunity to explore patterns at such scales.

Responding to pressures for more detailed information on literacy levels the 1971 census requested Welsh-speakers to state whether or not they could read and/or write the language. Not surprisingly, given the complexities of the issues involved, the census did not seek to determine proficiencies in reading and writing. The 1981 census continued with the categorization of Welsh-speakers according to sex, age and ability to read and/or write the language. Interestingly, and for the first time since 1921, language statistics for the 1981 census were not published for the communities (formerly parishes) of Wales. To assure continuity in their analyses of language change, Aitchison and Carter (1985) were obliged to re-create community data by aggregating records for constituent enumeration districts.

The 1991 Census

The 1991 Census of Population for Great Britain was taken on 21/22 April. Apart from published tabulations (e.g., county monitors), data have been made available in two datasets – Small Area Statistics (SAS) and Local Base Statistics (LBS). The former contain information for enumeration districts and aggregations thereof (e.g., wards), while the latter refer to wards and higher areal units (e.g., districts). The two datasets also differ in the number of items of information recorded, and in confidentiality restrictions (i.e., the minimum number of households and residents that there must be in an administrative unit before data are released without first being aggregated with other areas). Both datasets contain tables relating to the Welsh language. The tabulation used in this study is Table 67 from the SAS file. This contains 336 separate items of data. As in previous enumerations, the 1991 census details numbers of persons able to speak, read and write Welsh. However, there are differences in form. Firstly, the age-group subdivisions for the 1991 census are more numerous (20 in all); secondly, the categories relating to reading and writing Welsh are more detailed. Thus, in terms of language proficiency, it is possible to differentiate all combinations of ability to speak, read and write Welsh. Interestingly, the 1991 census did not ask whether or not persons were able to speak English. Thus, for the first time the number of Welsh monoglots cannot be determined.

Apart from changes in the precise presentation of the language statistics themselves, a further complication for those concerned with the analysis of language change arises as a result of differences in the definition of the base resident population for enumeration purposes.

The 1991 census considers the resident population to include:

(a)   Present residents
(b)   Absent residents (part of the household present)
(c)   Absent residents (wholly absent household – enumerated)
(d)   Absent residents (wholly absent household – imputed)

Given its treatment of absent households, this definition yields higher population figures than the definitions used in 1971 and 1981. The 1971 census covered those persons actually resident in households (including visitors), whereas in 1981 the base population related to persons 'usually resident' and therefore embraced just categories (a) and (b) above. These differences are of critical significance when it comes to precise calibrations of language trends, for they clearly influence both absolute numbers and the calculation of percentages. For purposes of comparison, it can be noted that the 1991 base population of Wales was 2,835,073. If the data are re-structured to accord with the 1971 and 1981 bases the total figures are 2,766,837 and 2,811,865 respectively. Unfortunately, apart from some limited data contained in the county monitors, the data relating to the Welsh language are only available at the 1991 population base. This makes it impossible to undertake any detailed analyses of language change at other than county level.

As has been noted, language data for the 1991 census are available for counties, districts, wards and enumeration districts. At the time the present analyses were undertaken, language data were not available at community level, although it would have been possible to aggregate constituent enumeration districts to derive such values. While this process was effected by Aitchison and Carter for the 1981 census in order to determine rates of change for the inter-censal periods between 1961 and 1981, such an exercise is not repeated here. The reasons for this are twofold. Firstly, the published data for enumeration districts are at the 1991 population base. As a consequence, direct comparisons cannot be made with previous censuses. This was not the case with the 1981 census; here data were also published at the 1971 base. Secondly, major changes in the boundaries of communities have taken place since the 1981 census, making the derivation of a constant spatial frame for the analysis of language change much more complex. Examination of administrative maps make it abundantly clear that quite major aggregations of communities would have to be made to secure a standard set of divisions (i.e., a spatial frame that could be used for the four censuses 1961–91). Together, these two limitations make it impossible to consider extending the previous the study of language change between 1961 and 1981 (Aitchison and Carter, 1985). Table 2.1 lists the numbers of wards, communities and enumeration districts that are contained in each of the county census files for 1991. Equivalent data for 1981 are also included for reference purposes. The tabulation confirms the major changes that have taken place in the numbers of communities, especially in Dyfed, Powys and Gwynedd. Although the numbers of wards have changed between 1981 and 1991, it is evident that they are not of the same order as for communities.

Table 2.1
Numbers of Wards, Communities and Enumeration Districts by Counties

County	Wards		Communities		Enumeration Districts	
	1981	1991	1981	1991	1981	1991
Clwyd	134	150	128	127	881	906
Dyfed	144	163	307	203	955	926
Gwent	93	111	76	98	925	944
Gwynedd	142	139	152	122	689	681
Mid Glamorgan	95	120	50	85	1170	1100
Powys	98	96	202	101	434	364
South Glamorgan	39	47	53	54	828	851
West Glamorgan	55	82	41	69	781	789
Total	800	908	1009	859	6663	6561

In this study the Welsh language maps for 1991 are prepared at the ward level. Figure 2.1 shows the spatial distribution of the 908 wards in Wales. The fact that the wards differ in areal size and shape is of some significance for it clearly affects not only the visual structure of the maps that are produced, but also impinges upon the interpretation of regional patterns. Of particular note in this regard are the differences in spatial detail for rural and urban areas. In the former, wards tend to be large in area and to have lower populations; this is especially true in upland regions. Urban areas are normally characterized by clusters of small wards with denser populations. Here it is possible to highlight more detailed local variations. These matters need not be elaborated upon further. Suffice it to say that geographers have long appreciated the importance of the scale issue in

Table 2.2
Wards by population size, 1991

Total population	Number of wards	% Number	% Population
Under 1000	88	9.7	2.4
1000–1499	140	15.4	6.4
1500–2499	278	30.6	19.1
2500–3499	127	14.0	13.3
3500–4499	93	10.2	13.0
4500–5499	65	7.2	11.4
5500 and over	117	12.9	34.4

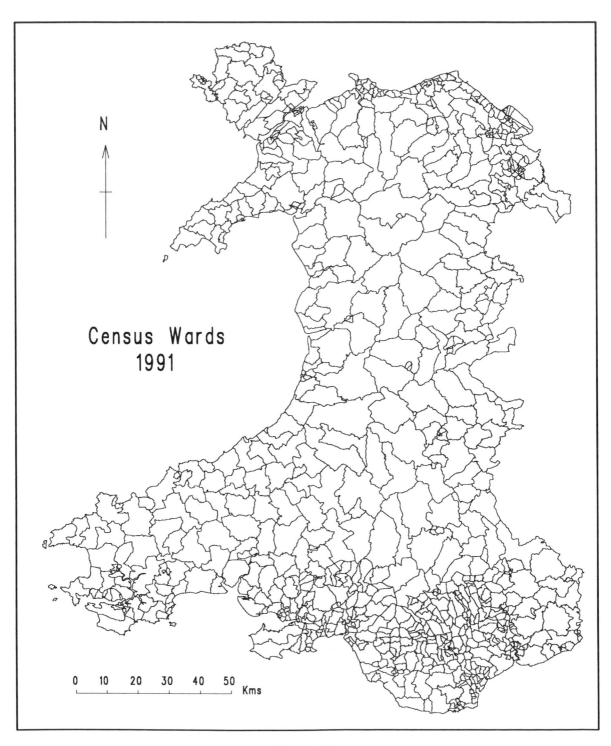

N

Census Wards
1991

0   10   20   30   40   50   Kms

Figure 2.1

cartographic analyses of this type. For purposes of reference, Table 2.2 lists the numbers and proportions of wards in terms of resident population size. The statistics serve to underline the degree of variation that exists within the set of Welsh wards. Thus, the 88 wards that have populations of less than 1,000 account for nearly 10 per cent of wards, but only contain 2.4 per cent of the Welsh population. At the other extreme are wards with populations of over 5,000 residents. Such areas (117) comprise 12.9 per cent of all wards, but have over a third of the total population.

Language Mapping

Language maps can be prepared using a variety of numerical measures. Since these are of significance to the present study it is appropriate to comment on the differing approaches that have been adopted. Of particular relevance in this regard is the distinction between absolute and relative values. Four basic treatments of the data can be distinguished:

(a) Absolute values
The raw statistics recorded by the census can be mapped directly as absolute values. In this case, proportional symbols (e.g., circles) can for instance be used to display the size of particular language features (e.g., numbers of Welsh-speakers).

(b) Relative values
While absolute values are of interest, it is often appropriate to express such data as percentages or ratios. Maps depicting the percentage of the resident population in an area that are able to speak Welsh are of this type. So too are maps showing densities (e.g., numbers of Welsh-speakers per km^2).

(c) Measures of change
Absolute and relative values can also be used to capture trends or changes over time. Various possibilities exist here. One approach is simply to determine the differences in absolute values between time t1 and time t2. Needless to say such values can be either positive, negative, or can show no change. Another approach is to chart differences in percentages or ratios (i.e., relative values) between t1 and t2. Finally, it is possible to calculate percentage rates of change over a period of time. In this case, absolute values at t2 can be expressed as ratios of values at t1. When considering these various approaches to the measurement of change it is to be appreciated that they can yield very differing interpretations. A simple example serves to illustrate the point. Table 2.3 records the total resident populations and numbers of Welsh-speakers for 1971 and 1981 in the community of Caron Uwch Clawdd (Tregaron). The figures show that the Welsh-speaking population increased during the decade by 23 or 12.1 per cent (percentage rate of change). However, whereas in 1971 the proportion of the population able to speak Welsh was 92.7 per cent (190 out of 205), in 1981 it had fallen to 81 per cent (213 out of 263). The percentage difference here is -11.7 per cent (92.7 − 81.0). The reason for this seemingly incongruous situation is of course that the percentage differences also take into account changes in the

19

number of non-Welsh-speakers in the area concerned. In this case a high in-migration of English monoglots diluted the relative strength of the language in the community.

Table 2.3
Total population over three years of age and
Welsh-speakers in Caron Uwch Clawdd

	1971	1981
Total resident population	205	263
Welsh-speakers	190	213

One final issue needs to be addressed before moving on to examine more substantive issues, and this is the nature of the questions asked in the census, and the likely quality of responses. Of particular concern here is the basic question on the census form – 'Does the person speak Welsh?' – and associated questions concerning reading and writing. Three problems arise.

Firstly, it is possible, though now, given the publicity which has surrounded the language issue, unlikely, that the question could be interpreted as a request concerning usage rather than fluency. That is the 'does' in the question, rather than the expected 'can', could be interpreted to mean 'What language do you usually use?' rather than 'Can you speak Welsh?'. Significantly, in Scotland and Northern Ireland the census question uses the word 'can'.

A second issue is that there is no measure of the degree of fluency which defines a Welsh-speaker; the interpretation is left to the individual completing the form and a wide variation is possible. The standard response has been to argue that variation will be equally distributed and, therefore, will not affect mapped distributions. But in 1991 a new problem has arisen. A considerable number of monoglot English-speaking parents have completed the census form on behalf of their children. Those children may be attending bilingual schools or be having Welsh lessons at school. There seems little doubt that such parents can easily exaggerate the fluency of their children and return them as Welsh-speakers, even though their grasp of the language may be rudimentary.

Finally, the question 'Do you understand Welsh?' is not asked. Evidence suggests that if this question were to be posed then the numbers would be much higher than those indicating that they are able speak Welsh.

Having elaborated upon these mapping and associated methodological issues the basis has been set for a consideration of the changing geography of the Welsh language. Chapter 3 provides a broad historical introduction and identifies the major forces and trends that affected the status and distribution of the language up until the 1961 census. This is followed by an examination of changes during the critical period 1961–81 (chapter 4). Chapter 5 looks more closely at the 1980s, drawing heavily on selected case studies of language change in rural and urban Wales. Chapter 6 charts contemporary language patterns through a more detailed, and strongly map-based study of the 1991 census, and highlights more recent trends. Finally, chapter 7 reflects on the future of the language.

CHAPTER 3

The Welsh Language and its Development: A Historical Overview

Although the statistical and cartographic analyses which form the heart of this study are primarily concerned with the period after the Second World War, and especially the three decades 1961 to 1991, it is appropriate to preface the discussion with a brief review of the major forces and events that have shaped the changing geography of the language in Wales up to the beginning of the 1960s.

The Welsh language is derived from what is called by linguists Common Celtic, itself a derivative from an Indo-European root. From their heartland in Central Europe the Celtic peoples spread in pre-Roman times to occupy most of Western Europe. Eventually, however, with the expansion of the Roman Empire, Celtic was replaced in all but the peripheral regions of Europe by Romance languages (Germanic regions apart). In these outlying imperial margins two branches of Celtic emerged – Brittonic (P Celtic) which characterized much of Britain, and Goidelic (Q Celtic) which was the language of Ireland. Presumably Brittonic remained the language of southern Britain during the Roman occupation, but the question as to whether a Celtic or Romance language would have succeeded in that area was pre-empted by the Anglo-Saxon invasions and the introduction of a Germanic language. One consequence of these folk movements was a reciprocal or counter invasion of north-west France from Cornwall and Wales. This was to result in the dominance there of the Breton language – a Brittonic successor.

The eastward press of the Anglo-Saxon peoples eventually led to the isolation of the Celtic-speaking populations, with those living in what is now Wales separated from their counterparts in Cornwall and in the north (Cumbria and Strathclyde). But, as Davies has argued,

> . . .we do not have to subscribe to the old cliché that the battles of Dyrham and Chester, c. 577 and 616 respectively, cut off the British of the South from those of the North to recognise that the English settlement over much of south western Britain had a politically and culturally confining effect. (Davies, 1982, 112)

Locked as they were in their remote strongholds, the Celts were called 'the strangers' by the Saxons (W(e)alas or Welsh; see Davies, J. 1990, 70). In their own terminology however they were 'the compatriots' (Y Cymry) and they spoke 'Cymraeg'.

At the end of the eighth century this cultural divide was given formal expression in the landscape when Offa, king of the growing power of Mercia, built the dyke or earthwork which now bears his name. To cross Offa's Dyke was to become in later days the symbol of leaving one's compatriots and entering the land of the English. The boundary which it constituted cannot be taken as a contemporary language divide however, for Welsh is recorded as having been spoken in Hereford and Shropshire even in modern times. Be that as it may, the effect of the dyke must have been greatly to accentuate differences, and it is certainly feasible to adopt it as a starting point for any discussion of language history. It serves as a base line from which to chart the slow and complex westward retreat of the Welsh language.

The first major episode in that retreat, and the one which brought English significantly beyond Offa's Dyke, was the Anglo-Norman invasion of Wales, beginning about 1070. Its ultimate impact is effectively measured by the distribution of one of its introductions, the system of manorial cultivation based on open-field agriculture. This system established itself most intensively along the coastal lowland regions of south Wales – southern Gwent, the Vale of Glamorgan, peninsular Gower and south Pembroke. The whole of the border lowland showed the same pattern of occupation with penetration along the valleys of the Usk, Wye and Severn. In the north the distribution was confined mainly to the east of the river Dee, with but occasional occurrences to the west. Beyond these areas the Anglo-Norman castle towns must also be regarded as forward bases of Anglicization.

The problem central to any investigation of subsequent retreat is not so much the absence of reliable data but the lack of any data at all. The most extensive discussion of the language in the period between the Norman incursion and the Act of Union is to be found in Llinos Beverly Smith's study, *Pwnc yr Iaith yng Nghymru 1282–1536* (Smith, L. B., 1986). She indicates how at the beginning of the period Welsh remained spoken to the limits of Offa's Dyke and, indeed, beyond.

> Ond yn y drydedd ganrif ar ddeg yr oedd acenion y Gymraeg yn berffaith hyglyw ar hyd y ffin â Lloegr. [But in the thirteenth century Welsh speech was clearly to be heard all along the English border.]

and . . .

> Y mae mwy nag un awgrym bod poblogaeth Gymraeg ei hiaith mewn rhanbarth mor ddwyreiniol â swydd Henffordd ar ddiwedd y bedwaredd ganrif ar ddeg ac wedyn. [There is more than one suggestion of Welsh-speakers in an area as far east as Herefordshire at the end of the fourteenth century and later.] (Smith, 1986, 4)

Even so, the inroads of the Anglo-Normans and their followers became more and more significant.

> Mae'n bur debyg, er enghraifft, mai'r Saesneg oedd iaith y gwladychwyr a ddaeth yn sgil goresgyniad y Normaniaid cynnar ac mai honno oedd yr iaith a gyflwynwyd ganddynt i

Fro Morgannwg a deheudir Penfro. [It is certain, for example, that English was the language of the settlers who followed the early Norman invasion and that English was the language which they introduced to the Vale of Glamorgan and south Pembrokeshire.] (Smith, 1986, 8)

This was particularly significant after the Edwardian conquest of Wales when –

Daeth ton newydd o deuluoedd estron, yn hanu o siroedd Caer a Chaerhirfryn, Caerefrog, Henffordd a Chaerwrangon, i ymsefydlu yn y bwrdeisdrefi newydd ac yn rhai o ardaloedd gwledig y gogledd-ddwyrain, a dichon iddynt hwythau ddwyn eu hiaith hefyd i'r mannau hynny. [There came a new wave of foreign families, from Cheshire and Lancashire, Yorkshire, Herefordshire and Worcestershire, to settle in the new boroughs and in some of the rural areas of the north-east, and probably they too brought their language to those areas.] (Smith, 1986, 8)

Whilst these trends and movements are significant, it does not mean that in the areas affected by Anglicizing influences Welsh was not present, or indeed that it was in decline. Even if the early burgess lists suggest the Anglicization of the towns, later listings indicate that the Welsh reasserted themselves (Carter, 1989). Moreover, as Llinos Smith points out, at no time was there any feeling that Welsh was in peril, and she notes that when the chronicler Ranulph Hegden, in the middle of the fourteenth century, listed the characteristics of the Welsh, there was no need to mention language but rather such things as dress, customs and diet. Again, at the time of the Glyndŵr uprising, only one chronicler refers to the language, namely Adda of Brynbuga who wrote –

. . . ac wedi derbyn pardwn gan y Saeson, bradychwyd Owain gan y Cymry, ac aethant yn ôl i'w cartrefi mewn cyni eithriadol, a chawsant yr hawl i ddefnyddio'r iaith Gymraeg er bod y Saeson wedi penderfynu ei dileu. Ond parodd yr Hollalluog, Brenin y Brenhinoedd, bod yr ordeiniad hwn yn cael ei ddymchwel ar ddeisyfiad y darostyngedig. [And having been pardoned by the English, Owain was betrayed by the Welsh, and they returned to their homes in great sorrow and obtained the right to use the Welsh language though the English had decided to eliminate it. But the Almighty, King of Kings caused this order to be overthrown on the petition of those in subjection.] (Smith, 1986, 26–7)

There was certainly a diminution in the dominance of Welsh in the areas settled by the Anglo-Normans, but perhaps the critical damage was not in the restriction of geographical extent but in the limitation of domain and consequent loss of status. To a great degree a distinctive legal system rather than a language was seen as the symbol of national identity at a time when kingdoms were being formed often out of amalgamations of ethnically contrasted territories. But Welsh law was essentially customary and within Wales the formal language of administration on such documents as treaties or charters was either Latin or French. With time, however, English was more and more used. Eventually it asserted itself as the language of formal documentation. This had the serious consequence of displacing Welsh from possible use in such transactions and effectively eliminating it from one of the most significant of domains. That, rather than any retreat in distribution, was the major setback for the language and a crucial step on what might have been its degradation to a patois.

Ai tynged anorfod yr iaith oedd iddi sichrau ei lle yn gyfrwng llên a diwylliant a bywyd ysbrydol y genedl heb ddatblygu'n iaith ddogfen a threfn ac ai cyn yr Uno y seliwyd ei ffawd? [Was it the inevitable fate of the language to ensure its place as the medium of the literature, culture and spiritual life of the nation but without its developing as the language of documentation and administration, and was its fate sealed before the Union?] (Smith, 1986, 31)

Thus, there ultimately followed from the proscription of Welsh from legal and administration affairs, a growing emphasis on language as the significant criterion of difference. R. R. Davies comments in the introductory chapter to his book *The Age of Conquest. Wales 1063–1415* (1991), that language was becoming one of the badges of national identity:

Those who did not speak Welsh (W. anghyfiaith) were immediately designated as aliens (W. estron); so it was that the English came to be branded as 'a foreign alien tongued people' (W. estron genedl anghyfiaith). (Davies, 1991, 17)

By the end of the period which the book considers, the failure of the Glyndŵr revolt

meant that the prospect of unitary native rule and political independence were gone for good. If the Welsh were to survive as a people, they would henceforth have to cultivate and sustain their identity, as in the past, by other means. (Davies, 1991, 465)

The 'other means' became the critical issue, for with the elimination of political identity, and the destruction of legal and administrative systems such as they were (which the Act of Union was finally to consummate), then language, and the literary tradition which was its highest expression, remained as the most significant hallmarks of Welshness. It might well be that one of the explanations of the unexpected survival of Welsh, as compared with Scots Gaelic and Irish, was that the other two Celtic peoples retained elements of separate legal, administrative and political systems as expressions of identity: Wales had nothing but the language.

Professor Rees Davies has described Wales during the Middle Ages as

an ill-assorted jigsaw of private lordships and royal shires, lacking all unity in law and government. It was treated, in effect, as a collection of colonial annexes dependent on the Crown and the higher aristocracy of England. (Davies, 1991, 461–2)

But once a United Kingdom was being created then that situation was totally unacceptable to the English crown. The Act of Union which ended it had inevitable repercussions on the language which had become the most tangible symbol of difference.

Under the Welsh house of Tudor the formal and complete association of Wales with England was accomplished by 'An Act for Laws and Justice to be ministered in Wales in like form as it is in this Realm' – the Act of Union as it has subsequently, if not properly, been called. The Welsh language was not formally proscribed by the Act, though by implication its demise was seen as something to be desired:

> And also by cause that the people of the same dominion have and do daily use a speech nothing like or consonant to the natural mother tongue used within this realm some rude and ignorant people have made distinction and diversity between the King's subjects of this Realm and his subjects of the said dominion and Principality of Wales. Whereby great discord variance debate division murmur and sedition have grown between his said subjects . . . his highness therefore minding and intending to reduce them to perfect order notice and knowledge of the laws . . . and utterly to extirpate all and singular the sinister usages and customs differing . . . his said country or dominion of Wales shall stand and continue from henceforth incorporated united and annexed to and with his realm of England.

The critical phrase here is 'to extirpate all and singular the sinister usages and customs differing'. Although it applied directly to law, it also unequivocally implied a process of cultural assimilation and hence of language erosion. This was reinforced by the provision that 'from henceforth no Person or Persons that use the Welsh Speech or Language shall have or enjoy any Manner Office or Fees within the Realm of England, Wales or Other the King's Dominion' (Bowen, 1908).

The Act of Union by making the English language the sole language of government and law finally and formally abstracted a domain of use from Welsh which had effectively been lost long before. But to that it is possible to add another and less tangible reduction. If Welsh were not to be used in a significant formal context then it meant, too, that its use in informal contexts would diminish. Inevitably, if the Welsh gentry wished to participate in public life then that participation would be in English and the language of polite society, if such it can be called, would also be English. There followed the conviction that Welsh was the language of the barbarous past, English the language of the civilized future. 'The increasing tendency among churchmen to ascribe a superior status to the English tongue was . . . a growing problem' (Jenkins, 1978, 9). Geraint Jenkins notes that until 'the end of the seventeenth century, the survival of the Welsh language had been largely the result of the efforts of the Welsh clergy and their flocks' but that alliance was under threat. In 1717 an Anglican minister of the diocese of St David's 'claimed that some of his fellow clergy, ensnared in the web of Anglicization, were too haughty and "puffed up" to preach in Welsh to monoglot parishioners' (Jenkins, 1978, 9). Even

> . . .the attitude of charitable bodies towards the Welsh language was an open secret: it

26

was, at best, a nuisance, and, at worst, a pernicious relic of barbarism. It is plain that the policy of the Welsh Trust and the SPCK of distributing religious literature in Welsh was essentially a short-term expedient calculated to save the souls of those monoglot Welshmen who were poised on the brink of everlasting damnation; they believed their more enduring function to be the rearing of a new generation of English speakers in the network of charity schools which they had established in the Principality. (Jenkins, 1987, 37)

But religious attitudes that souls were best saved in English were the mirror of those growing in secular society, expressed in their most extreme form by William Richards of Helmdon in his *Wallography* of 1682.

The Native Gibberish is usually prattled throughout the whole of Taphydome, except in their Market Towns, whose Inhabitants being a little raised, and (as it were) pufft up into Bubbles, above the ordinary scum, do begin to despise it . . . 'Tis usually cashier'd out of Gentlemen's Houses . . . the Lingua will be Englishd out of Wales. (Richards, 1682, 63)

In a more balanced summary Geraint Jenkins writes in relation to writers in Welsh –

Authors knew that there had been a time when the gentry's pride included a delight in Welshness and a proper regard for the language; but it was all too evident now that their pride was being shaped and dominated by the values of their English counterparts. (Jenkins, 1987, 260–1)

There can be distilled from these various comments another critical loss of domain. The eighteenth century was the Age of Enlightenment, the time which saw the widespread influence of scholars such as Descartes, Leibnitz and Newton. Not only did natural science experience a major efflorescence, but in all the professions issues were scrutinized free from the trammels of traditional religious orthodoxy. Above all, it was the age of science: the Royal Society had been founded in 1660. But these new ideas were to permeate society through the educated gentry and down the urban hierarchy. In brief, the diffusion of the new ideas was directly related to social standing and to settlement size, and in that way they were bound into social class and the English language. Thus science, too, became a domain in which Welsh took little part, although there were the obvious exceptions, most notably Edward Lhuyd and the Morris brothers (Cylch y Morrisiaid).

It is apparent that in the foregoing discussion little has been written about geographical distribution, largely because little can be written. There is no evidence of any clear retreat. Even William Richards of Helmdon referred to the *whole* of Wales in his animadversion. Perhaps the best summary is provided by Prys Morgan, for in considering the distribution in the eighteenth century he writes,

in that sense Welsh was as healthy as any other language in Europe; left in total isolation, its future would be secure. Yet its status was low, hardly more than that of a patois or peasant language, rescued from dissolving into mutually incomprehensible dialects by the excellent Welsh of the Elizabethan Anglican liturgy, the Bible and the supporting homilies and apologetic literature. Welsh was used remarkably rarely as a written language, and it was not taught to more than a handful in any methodical way. (Morgan, 1981, 68)

Further, but not totally unproblematical, insights into the geographical distribution of the Welsh language at this time can be gained from the map of non-Celtic place-names before 1715 (Figure 3.1) constructed by A. J. Parkinson for Peter Smith's *Houses of the Welsh Countryside* (Smith, P., 1975, 340). It serves as one indicator of the strength of the penetration of English throughout the Marcher regions of south Wales and the borderland.

There can be no doubt that the changes taking place during the eighteenth century were to have a major impact upon Wales, upon Welshness and upon the language.

In the Methodist view of Welsh history, the eighteenth century is the century of the Great Revival . . . One of the earliest attempts to define this cultural revival was by William Roberts 'Nefyn' in 1852. In his *Crefydd yr Oesoedd Tywyll* (Religion of the Dark Ages), he called it the *Cyffrawd Cymreigyddol* (Movement of Welshness). (Morgan, 1981, 13)

It was characterized by the abandonment of what had become traditional culture based on the myths of Gildas and Geoffrey of Monmouth, and of 'the rise of a more serious, self-conscious Welshness based on books, eisteddfodau and literary or debating societies' (Morgan, 1981, 13). Many regarded with despair the loss of the past, most notably epitomized in Ellis Wynne's *Gweledigaethau y Bardd Cwsg* (Visions of the Sleeping Bard), but the renaissance of the eighteenth century encompassed a unique revival of things Welsh. As John Davies writes,

Yn wir, llwyddwyd i ailddiffinio Cymreictod gan beri amheuon ynglŷn â hawl y rhai nad anwesent y diwylliant hwnnw i gael eu hystyried yn etifeddion gwir draddodiadau Cymru. [Indeed, they succeeded in redefining Welshness, causing doubt concerning the right of those who did not embrace that culture to be considered heirs of the true traditions of Wales.] (Davies, 1990, 300)

Without question, one of the greatest influences in the preservation and extension of the language during the eighteenth century were the circulating schools initiated by Griffiths Jones, Vicar of Llanddowror. His motivation was the saving of souls, not the safeguarding of the language. The scheme was based on itinerant teachers who stayed at a location for about three months to teach reading so that the Bible was made accessible. As John Davies writes,

Yn *Welch Piety* ceir manylion o flwyddyn i flwyddyn am nifer y disgyblion. Gelli eu dehongli i olygu fod dros 200,000 o bobl, bron hanner poblogaeth Cymru, wedi mynychu'r ysgolion erbyn 1771, blwyddyn marwolaeth Griffith Jones. [In *Welch Piety*

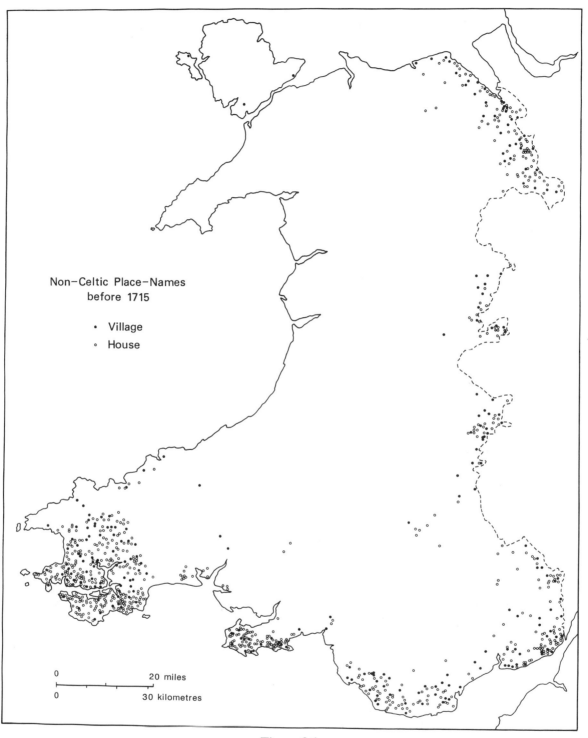

Non-Celtic Place-Names
before 1715

• Village
∘ House

0   20 miles

0   30 kilometres

Figure 3.1

there are details from year to year of the number of pupils. It is possible to estimate that over 200,000, almost half the population of Wales, attended the schools by 1771, the year of Griffith Jones' death.] (Davies, J., 1990, 295)

David Williams's summary of Griffith Jones's work remains appropriate –

He helped to make the Welsh a literate nation, and his circulating schools were the most important experiment in religious education in the eighteenth century, not only in Wales but in Britain and all the British dominions. (Williams, D. 1950, 147)

But the renaissance was a great deal more than a Methodist movement and was expressed through such aspects as the preparation of dictionaries of the language, the revival of eisteddfodau, the growth of Welsh debating societies, and the rise of scholarly history to replace the old myths. It even generated the inventions of Iolo Morganwg. However, one feature stands out. The movements of the eighteenth century deepened and enriched the domains in which Welsh was already used, and it conserved the language because of that; but it did not extend the domains, and that was to be crucial in the next century.

The earliest map of the distribution of the language is that for 1750 constructed by Rees Pryce (1978a; 1978b). The data on which this is based are derived from the returns of curates, vicars and rectors throughout Wales concerning the use of Welsh and/or English in services. This information allows a distinction to be made between areas where services were Welsh, mainly Welsh, bilingual, mainly English and English. In considering the territorial domination of Welsh, Pryce writes,

Before the early industrialization of north-east Wales and the later growth of metallurgical and mining industries in the south, on the evidence of the visitation returns Wales was overwhelmingly a Welsh speaking country. (Pryce, 1978a, 241)

And again,

In south-east Wales the Welsh-speaking heartland extended right through the western half of the county of Monmouth to reach the River Usk. Moreover, the greater part of Glamorganshire was then an integral part of Welsh Wales. (Pryce, 1978a, 244)

The conclusion from an examination of Pryce's map (Figure 3.2) is that the completely Anglicized areas were very restricted and that no major inroads into Welsh Wales had been made since the Middle Ages. Although Pryce allows for some change in a narrow zone which he characterized as bilingual, he accepts that 'in the county of Radnor, east Monmouthshire, Gower and south Pembrokeshire, even in the mid-eighteenth century English had been the sole language of the people for many generations' (Pryce, 1978a, 247). These were, of course, the Englishries of the Middle Ages. The critical point which

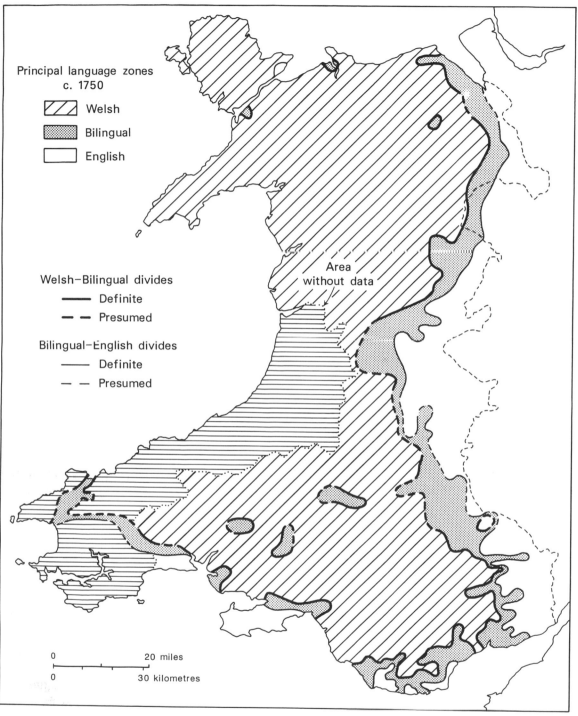

Principal language zones
c. 1750

Welsh

Bilingual

English

Welsh–Bilingual divides
——— Definite
— — Presumed

Bilingual–English divides
——— Definite
— — Presumed

Area
without data

0   20 miles
0   30 kilometres

After W.T.R. Pryce 1978

Figure 3.2

emerges, therefore, is not the geographical displacement of Welsh during the long period from the Act of Union to the middle of the eighteenth century, but rather the crucial and progressive limitation of domains in which it was used and the concomitant restriction of status. The domains were never purely domestic, that is confined to the hearth, and the language never suffered from such limitation, largely due to the translation of the Bible and the religious movements of the eighteenth century. But whereas these traditional domains of hearth, chapel, literature and all its associated activities as in eisteddfodau, and it must be added of agriculture, remained secure, the newer domains of what can be called 'polite society', and of science, together with the long-standing domains of law, administration and government remained essentially English. Thus the dilution of language which had occurred largely by the Anglicization of the gentry, and in the towns, together with domain limitation which was intimately associated with it, left the language particularly vulnerable to the massive transformations of the next century.

It is an impossible task to present a brief resumé of language change during the nineteenth century. Fortunately there are two major studies, that by Ieuan Gwynedd Jones on 'Language and Community in Nineteenth Century Wales' which was included in his book of essays on *Mid-Victorian Wales* (Jones, 1992), and that by Hywel Teifi Edwards on 'Y Gymraeg yn y Bedwaredd Ganrif ar Bymtheg' which appeared in Volume 2 of *Cof Cenedl* (Edwards, 1987). In addition, local studies have become much richer and one of the latest and best is *Oes y Byd i'r Iaith Gymraeg* by Sian Rhiannon Williams (1992), a study of Welsh in the industrial area of Monmouthshire during the nineteenth century. Alongside the richness of those works only a rudimentary review can be undertaken here, but with a continued emphasis on the combined theme of domains of use and social status.

The complexity, which makes a constrained discussion of language change difficult, derives from the massive economic changes associated with industrialization and the related transformation of the population distribution. In simplest terms the total population of Wales increased from 587,245 at the 1801 census to 2,012,876 at the 1901 census, although some boundary changes were involved. Glamorgan returned a population of 70,879 in 1801 but by 1901 this had increased elevenfold to 859,931. In contrast, by 1871 all the rural counties were experiencing actual population loss; the rural depopulation which was to be characteristic for one hundred years had set in. Such change inevitably had a major impact upon language distribution, particularly in the build-up of Welsh-speaking populations in Glamorgan, Carmarthenshire and Monmouthshire, as well as in the counties of Denbigh and Flint. But it is essential to stress one point. Much of the movement was internal migration and, especially in the south, migration from England only became significant at the end of the century. Even so, closely linked to migration was an increasing ease of movement which was brought about by the new railway system. The isolation of Wales, upon which the survival of the language had to a degree been reliant, was being broken down.

Inevitably much of the discussion of the language in the nineteenth century centres on the Report of the Commissioners of Inquiry into the State of Education in Wales of 1847, 'Brad y Llyfrau Gleision' (the Treachery of the Blue Books). Again, there is an admirable exegesis by Ieuan Gwynedd Jones (1992). The reason for the reaction to the Report is quite clear. Industrialization and the business entrepreneur were creating new opportunities for the creation of wealth; and progress was defined in terms of material wealth. But the language in the domains of technology and business, successors of science and administration, was English. Without fluency in that language Welsh people would remain isolated and poor. But further, as has been already suggested, English was the language of 'polite society', so it was thought the Welsh would also be removed from the civilizing influences of the new bourgeoisie. The commissioners were unable to comprehend that a different culture, possibly with different values, could exist within the bounds of a United Kingdom. Wales was therefore perceived as backward and the reason manifestly rested with the language which isolated the population from the benefits of 'progress'. There is little space here for extended quotation and analysis, but one extract from I. G. Jones's study clearly indicates the central issue:

> In the minds of the Commissioners and of their political masters the two [the Welsh language and Nonconformity] were connected, and it was in the connection that the evil resided. The language was the major isolating factor in the life of the ordinary people: it isolated the Welshman from all influences except those which arose within his class. He lived 'in an underworld of his own', as Lingen [one of the Commissioners] puts it; 'a disastrous barrier to all moral progress', as Symonds [another Commissioner] expressed it. According to Lingen it distorted the class system, by isolating the mass of the people from their natural leaders, and compelled the ordinary man to the life of a helot or labourer; 'they are never masters . . . never found at the top of the social scale', either in town or country, lacking the entrepreneurial spirit, initiating nothing new, no new enterprise or source of profit or means of social advance. (Jones, 1992b, 137)

From the above it is possible to derive two fundamental limitations of the language perceived by Victorian society. The first was the exclusion of Welsh from the new and developing domains of technology, a successor of science, and of business. As David Davies of Llandinam, 'the exemplar of the self-made man', is quoted as saying in *Y Geninen* —

> Os ydych am barhau i fwyta bara tywyll a gorwedd ar wely gwellt, gwaeddwch chwi eich gorau, 'Oes y byd i'r iaith Gymraeg': ond os ydych chwi yn chwennych bwyta bara gwyn a chig eidon rost, mae yn rhaid i chwi ddysgu Saesneg. [If you wish to continue to eat black bread and lie on straw beds, carry on shouting 'Long life to the Welsh language'. But if you wish to eat white bread and roast beef you must learn English.] (Jones, 1992a, 70)

The second perceived limitation is a derivative from the English character of bourgeois society. The nineteenth century was a period when there was a massive extension in the array of social classes, not only due to the development of industrial skills, but also, and in many ways more significantly, due to the growth of clerical work. Each stratum of the class system sought to distance itself from that below and associate itself with that above. There were Pooters in Wales! The language became an integral part of that process, of the way to ape a superior social class. To speak English, preferably with an accent akin to that of genteel English society, became an ideal to be pursued. Welsh became a language which children need not acquire, indeed they were better without it since it carried at least an implication of exclusion from the higher reaches of society. Moreover, time could be devoted to more profitable ends, for Welsh had no apparent economic value. The result was symbolized by the 'Welsh Not' and in practice produced a secular education which was English directed.

But there was also another domain in which the language was to lose relevance, even if only to a degree. The radical reaction of Welsh Nonconformity had been embodied in support for the Liberal Party; Nonconformity and Liberalism were inextricably associated and the Welsh language was the matrix of that association. But by the end of the nineteenth century and the beginning of the twentieth much of radical opinion was turning to socialism, and to a socialism which saw itself as international and cosmopolitan, and so removed from purely Welsh traditions.

> From 1911 onwards socialism and the new miners' union were becoming the new religion. The language of socialism was English . . . To abandon Welsh became not only a valuational but also a symbolic rejection and affirmation. (Jones, 1992a, 78)

That was a rejection of the Liberal/Nonconformist past, an affirmation of a secular and English-based movement. Thus yet another domain was lost to the Welsh language as political philosophy and action became rooted in English. It was in English that the confrontation between Labour and Conservative, the parties of the new era, was to be conducted. So it was in the greatly burgeoning field of local government, partly as a result of the ancient proscriptions, partly because of the new party systems.

The immediate assumption from this catalogue of problems, curtailed as it is, would be one of marked language decline. But, superficially at least, nothing could be further from the truth. The end of the century was the period when the highest *numbers* of Welsh speakers were recorded; the maximum was 977,366 reached in 1911, although a higher *proportion*, effectively half the population, was returned in 1901 when the number was 929,824. Hywel Teifi Edwards adds to these figures the fact that in 1896 there were 32 periodicals and 25 newspapers published in Welsh and that in 1886–7 Hughes and Son (publishers at Wrexham) gave evidence before the Cross Commission (on elementary education) that at least £100,000 was spent annually on literature in Welsh. He adds, 'dyna le i gredu, mae'n rhaid, fod diwedd y bedwaredd ganrif ar bymtheg yn Oes Aur yn hanes Cymreictod', (There is room to believe, certainly, that the end of the nineteenth century was a golden age in the history of Welshness), (Edwards, 1987, 122). This is the traditional view clearly set out by Professor K. O. Morgan in what is the definitive history of Wales at this period:

Welsh in the 1880s was securely based in terms of daily intercourse . . . Whatever its aesthetic or technical limitations, it had a clear capacity for growth – and as a medium for a significant mode of cultural expression, not merely as a peasant patois . . . Most important of all, Welsh was the language of contemporary argument and discussion. (Morgan, 1981, 21)

And again, during the 1880s 'dramatic transformations swept through the land which added up to a kind of national renaissance' which

expressed itself at the most popular grass roots level. The Welsh language in some ways proved more vigorous than ever in the years after 1880. It had new status and protection. In 1885 a group of cultured patriots . . . founded a Society for the Utilization of the Welsh Language. (Morgan, 1981, 95)

Moreover, all this was backed by, indeed was part of, what Morgan uses as his chapter heading – 'The growth of national consciousness'. It is usually symbolized in the founding of a national movement, Cymru Fydd, in 1866; a Young Wales movement parallel to those on the continent.

Given the general opinion of the time, and the characterization by historians since, that the turn of the century marked a 'Golden Age', then two basic questions arise. The first is, why was the condition of the language regarded so optimistically when all the evidence which has been presented would suggest the opposite? The second is, why did the twentieth century witness such an immediate and, indeed, drastic collapse?

Before seeking to answer these questions, one word of caution needs to be introduced. After referring to a Golden Age, Hywel Teifi Edwards adds:

Nid dyna'r gwir, wrth gwrs. Gwyddom, er bod nifer y Cymry Cymraeg rhwng 1871 a 1901 yn fwy nag y buasai erioed, ei fod fel canran o'r boblogaeth gyfan wedi gostwng yn gyson trwy gydol y ganrif. Amcangyfrifodd Thomas Darlington fod rhyw 587,245 yn byw yng Nghymru ym 1801 a bod 80% yn siarad Cymraeg. Erbyn 1841, yn ôl amcangyfrif Syr Thomas Phillips, roedd y boblogaeth yn 1,046,073 a 67% ohoni a siaradai'r iaith, ac er i Ernst Georg Ravenstein faentumio ym 1879 fod 71.2% o boblogaeth o 1,312,583 yn medru'r Gymraeg, erbyn troad y ganrif, fel y nodwyd roedd y canran wedi disgyn i 49.9. Buan y peidia ystadegau'r Gymraeg ar derfyn Oes Victoria â bod yn foddion llawenydd pan wynebir y caswir am dwf y boblogaeth rhwng 1801 a 1891.

[That was not true, of course, we know that although the number of Welsh-speakers between 1871 and 1901 was more than ever, the percentage had steadily declined during the century. Thomas Darlington estimated that 587,245 people lived in Wales in 1801 and that 80 per cent spoke Welsh. By 1841, according to the estimate of Sir Thomas Phillips, out of a population of 1,046,073, some 67 per cent were Welsh speaking, and although Ernst Georg Ravenstein maintained that in 1879 out of a population of 1,312,583 there were 71.2 per cent who spoke Welsh, by the end of the century, as has been noted, the percentage had fallen to 49.9. The statistics concerning the Welsh language at the end of the Victorian age soon cease to be a cause for rejoicing when faced with the unpalatable truth regarding the growth in population between 1801 and 1891.] (Edwards, 1987, 122)

Professor Edwards proceeds to demonstrate how rising numbers of Welsh-speakers constituted a falling proportion of the rapidly growing population. He notes the conclusion of J. C. Southall that whereas the 'clientele' of Welsh had risen by some 25 per cent between 1841 and 1871 it had remained much the same between 1876 and 1891, and that while Southall considered the century to be not 'wholly against Welsh', 'all the while . . . the nineteenth century was sharpening its knives, and gradually gathering strength, to dispute further advances' (Edwards, 1987, 123).

In Edwards's summary lie the answers to the two questions which were set out above. The growth of population had meant simply and directly the growth of the Welsh-speaking population. Moreover, until the end of the century most of the migrants to the coalfields of north and south came from the rural Welsh-speaking areas of Wales, rather than from England. And the main generator of growth was natural increase. In the five decades of the latter half of the nineteenth century, natural increase in Wales registered percentage gains of 12.3, 13.52, 14.73, 13.73 and 14.06 respectively. For the same decades migration actually registered percentage losses of 1.67, 3.82, 3.67, 1.13 and 0.53. The succeeding decade 1901–11 recorded a migration gain of 4.84 per cent, marking the late major phase of in-migration from England (Williams, J. 1985, 68). But a natural increase over most of the century, largely of Welsh families, produced the growth of Welsh-speaking numbers.

The consequence of internal migration and natural increase was one of the major phenomena of the nineteenth century, urban growth (Carter and Lewis, 1991). Certainly in their early stages these towns, and especially the urban villages, were predominantly Welsh speaking. This is one of the reasons why Gwyn A. Williams called Merthyr Tydfil the first Welsh town (Williams, 1966, 2). It is also the reason why Brinley Thomas has so cogently argued that industrialization and urbanization saved the Welsh language by giving it a new vitality as against decline, like Irish, to a remote western Gaeltacht (Thomas, 1987). In these towns and villages the stereotype of the chapel-going, choir-singing, and in the south, rugby-playing, Welshman (it was a time when stereotypes were male-derived) was founded. But it was the numbers that were the real basis for the optimism which sustained the idea of a Golden Age, especially perhaps amongst an élite which was somewhat removed from the realities of Anglicization. The most optimistic expression was that of D. Isaac Davies who published a book of essays in 1885 under the title *Yr Iaith Gymraeg, 1785, 1885, 1985! neu Tair Miliwn o Gymry Dwy-iaethawg mewn Can Mlynedd* (The Welsh Language, 1785, 1885, 1985! or Three Million Bilingual Welsh People in a Hundred Years). But as Southall was foresighted enough to realize, 'the knives were being sharpened'. All the problems of the loss of domains and the associated decline of social prestige were already apparent. Brinley Thomas was, of course, quite right when he argued

that a major cause of the decline of the Welsh language was the collapse of the Welsh economy after World War I . . . Because of the dazzling heights reached just before World War I, the subsequent fall was all the more disastrous. The class war in the coalfields intensified, and the clarion call was Marxist not Methodist. What the potato famine did to the Irish economy, the great depression did to the Welsh economy. In the twentieth century, economic and demographic contraction, the decline of nonconformity, severe unemployment and emigration . . . have been a curse to the language. (Thomas, 1987, 437)

But all these forces, to which rural depopulation must be added, were acting upon a condition which had been established and developed over the long period since the Anglo-Norman incursion; they acted upon a context long prepared and their impact was great because of that. By the end of the century the time has been reached when geographical data first became available and it is possible to turn to a review of the regional distribution of the language.

Figure 3.3 reproduces the situation in 1901 as mapped by W. T. R. Pryce (1978a). The map superimposes two evidential bases. The first is the percentage speaking Welsh at the 1901 census. These are on the census basis of the Rural and Urban districts, one which is necessarily crude and obscures finer detail. The second is the Welsh–bilingual–English divides which Pryce derived from the language used in Anglican Church services, and which he took to represent core, domain and sphere. Even by 1901 it is apparent that the significant lineaments of decline which have characterized the twentieth century were already evident. But before identifying them, and possibly overstressing them, it is pertinent to emphasize the strength of the core. There is a dominant and extensive area, virtually all of Wales, except for South Pembrokeshire, west of a line running north–south from the Conwy estuary to that of the Tawe, where over 90 per cent of the population spoke Welsh. The core was clear, unmistakable and strong.

Strong as it was, however, the core was also clearly being eroded at its edges. The whole of the classic Marcher area, along the English border to the east, and in the Vale of Glamorgan, Gower and South Pembrokeshire to the south revealed the considerable impact of an ancient Anglicization which was progressive in its character. As Pryce observes, 'the figures for Brecnockshire display the classic stages of language change . . . Welsh in 1801, bilingual in 1851 and substantially Anglicized by 1881'. The crucial zone was that identified by Pryce as bilingual, where the two languages were in contact. 'In effect, therefore, it seems that bilingualism was merely a stage in the process of Anglicization. Once a community became bilingual, the next generation failed to retain Welsh as a spoken language' (Pryce, 1978a, 5). This same pattern has been identified by Philip N. Jones by using *Baptist chapels as an index of cultural transition in the South Wales Coalfield before 1914* (1976). His work identifies three chronological phases 'during which the coalfield was transformed from a uniformly Welsh cultural area before 1860, through an intervening phase of linguistic heterogeneity, to a situation in the final phase after 1890, when the dominance of Welsh was restricted to the western section only'. He proposes a progressive 'rolling back' of Welsh from east to west, 'a rapid and regular process in which

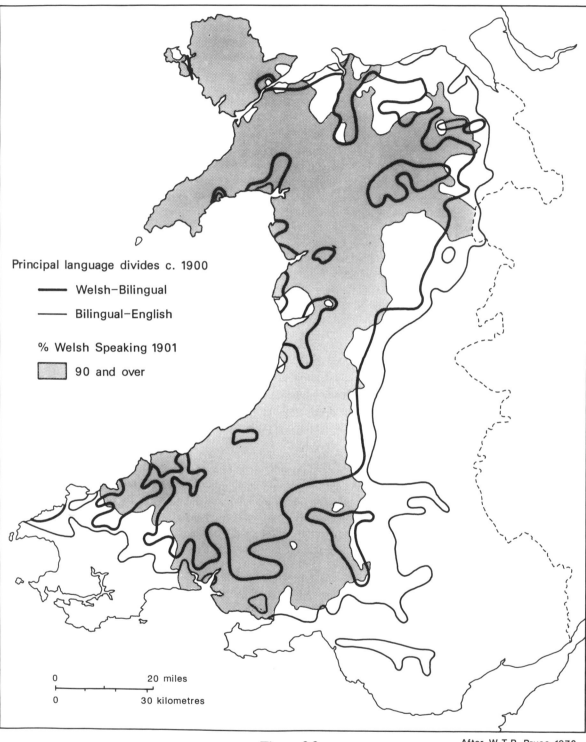

Principal language divides c. 1900

Welsh–Bilingual

Bilingual–English

% Welsh Speaking 1901

90 and over

0   20 miles

0   30 kilometres

Figure 3.3

After W.T.R. Pryce 1978

bilingualism was only a transient resting-place' (Jones, P. N. 1976, 347). And that was during the 'Golden Age' of the language.

The forces at work are difficult to identify from aggregate data. However, standard linguistic processes would suggest stages where codes are mixed, that is, English words or structures are used in Welsh speech, followed by code switching, where speakers of a minority language change for a variety of reasons into another language. But the bases of switching have been evident. These were largely related to motivation which was in turn linked to the loss of domains and status which this survey has traced. The young or their parents saw no advantage in the language and it was gradually lost. At the same time the predominant English bias of the education system meant that formal learning, too, diminished.

> There seems little doubt that in the promotion of English for supposedly secular needs, state education soon began to reflect what was then considered to be a popular aspiration. The policies adopted during the later decades of the nineteenth century meant that the children of Wales were to be eventually divorced from a close experiential knowledge of the language and culture of previous generations. (Pryce, 1987a, 28)

At this point it is necessary to observe that all the processes which were inimical to Welsh were at their most virulent where Welsh and English were in daily contact. Isolation had always been one of the major sustainers of Welsh. Industrialization, by increasing the mobility of populations (just as the railway provided the means), broke down that isolation, as did social upheavals like the First World War. But even so, until the coming of the mass media, direct contact had a strong geographical limitation and the pattern of language change can be discussed in the terms of a retreating frontier. But all this was beginning to change.

If the westward retreat of the language divide, albeit leaving some outliers, was apparent, so too was the characteristic pattern within the south Wales coalfield. Anglicization was greatest lower down the valleys, and to the east. It was spreading up-valley and westward, a process to be accelerated during the century. Even the incipient Anglicization of the north Wales coastline is apparent, revealed both by the church service data and the census figures. The beginnings of the axis of decline across Snowdonia from Conwy to Porthmadog is again suggested, as are fragments of diminution along the west coast. In brief, the great fault lines which were later to break up the core are just perceptible.

The basic features of the ensuing period of retreat are apparent in Figure 3.4 which maps the areas in which over 80 per cent of the population spoke Welsh in 1931 and 1951. Perhaps one aspect is unexpected in that there had been no significant westward retreat of the eastern 'frontier' with English. After the retreat in the nineteenth century there appears to have been a period of some stability with only marginal shifts. But that was probably as much a reflection of the very thinly inhabited mountain backbone on which the divide eventually came to rest. As that happened so the crucial areas of conflict switched to those

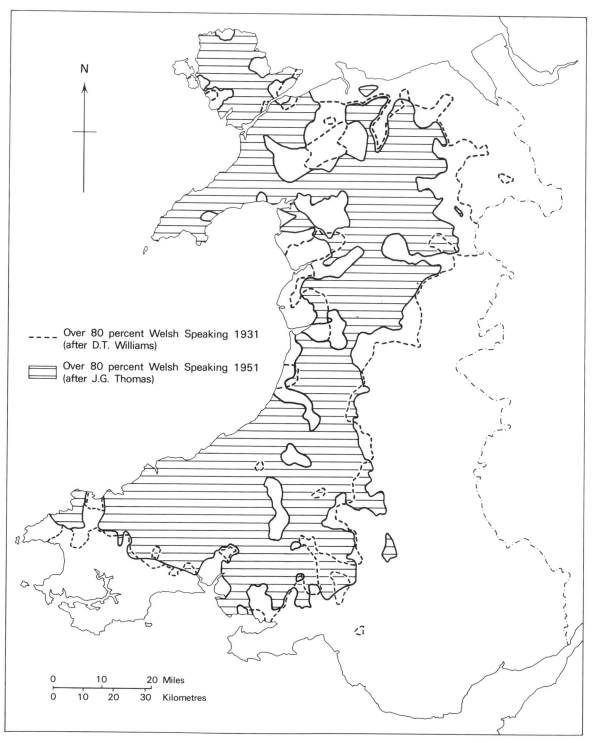

N

- - - - Over 80 percent Welsh Speaking 1931
(after D.T. Williams)

Over 80 percent Welsh Speaking 1951
(after J.G. Thomas)

0   10   20 Miles
0   10   20   30 Kilometres

Figure 3.4

Table 3.1
Percentage of population able to speak Welsh, 1901–1951 (pre-1974 counties)

	1901	1911	1921	1931	1951
Anglesey	91.7	88.7	84.9	87.4	79.8
Breconshire	45.9	41.5	37.2	37.3	30.3
Caernarfonshire	89.6	85.6	75.0	79.2	71.0
Cardiganshire	93.0	89.6	82.1	87.1	79.5
Carmarthenshire	90.4	84.9	82.4	82.3	77.3
Denbighshire	61.9	56.7	48.4	48.5	38.5
Flintshire	49.1	42.2	32.7	31.7	21.1
Glamorgan	43.5	38.1	31.6	30.5	20.3
Merioneth	93.7	90.3	82.1	86.1	75.4
Monmouthshire	13.0	9.6	6.4	6.0	3.5
Montgomeryshire	47.5	44.8	42.3	46.7	35.1
Pembrokeshire	34.4	32.4	30.3	30.6	26.9
Radnorshire	6.2	5.4	6.3	4.7	4.5
Wales	49.9	43.5	37.1	36.8	28.9

locations which have caused the greatest concern in more recent times, parts within the north and west, or *Y Fro Gymraeg* as that Welsh-speaking core came to be called. This is clearly seen in the mapping of the 1951 census returns by J. G. Thomas (Thomas, 1956, 1975). The area with over 90 per cent speaking Welsh, which had been a continuous block in 1901, had by the mid-century been broken down into a series of separated extents, and the area with over 80 per cent was attenuated and barely continuous. Some reservation is needed, however, since the larger units on which the data were available in 1901 might have exaggerated the solidarity of this western block.

The extent of the decline of the language in the first half of the twentieth century is shown in Table 3.1. As has been demonstrated, a whole nexus of socio-economic changes had reacted with domain limitation and status loss to produce a fifty-year period of catastrophic decline, all the more hurtful since it had followed so closely on what had been perceived as a golden age of renewal and opportunity. By 1961 the situation appeared parlous – it was to deteriorate even further in the decade that followed. Urgent action was needed – it was eventually forthcoming.

CHAPTER 4

The Critical Years: Language Change 1961–1981

Of all the events relating to the recent history of the Welsh language none is of more pivotal significance than the radio broadcast by Saunders Lewis in 1962. Entitled 'Tynged yr Iaith' (The Fate of the Language), it was an apocalyptic and trenchant lecture, designed to bring home to the people of Wales the full severity of the crisis facing the language. The celebrated polemic was an attempt to raise the Welsh from what he saw as apathy and an acceptance of inevitable loss.

> I shall presuppose that the figures which will shortly be published [the 1961 census] will shock and disappoint those of us who consider that Wales without the Welsh language will not be Wales. I shall also presuppose that Welsh will end as a living language, should the present trend continue, about the beginning of the twenty-first century. (Lewis, 1973)

Lewis's greatest condemnation was not of the external English but of the neglect, indeed the clear opposition, by Welsh people themselves –

> Naturally there would be a few muttered curses from clerks looking for a dictionary and from girl typists who were learning to spell, but the Civil Service has long since learned to accept revolutionary changes in the British Empire as part of the daily routine. The opposition – harsh, vindictive and violent – would come from Wales. (Lewis, 1973, 137)

And again –

> In my opinion, if any kind of self-government for Wales were obtained before the Welsh language was acknowledged and used as an official language in local authority and state administration in the Welsh-speaking parts of our country, then the language would never achieve official status at all, and its demise would be quicker than it will under English rule. (Lewis, 1973, 141)

Lewis set out no coherent policy, other than a demand for Welsh in public life, but his lecture led directly to the founding of Cymdeithas yr Iaith Gymraeg in 1962 (Tudur, 1989) and opened up a new era in the struggle to maintain and advance the language.

As it turned out the results of the 1961 census were not as cataclysmic as Lewis had feared. Certainly, the decline continued, but given what had happened previously it could hardly be described as dramatic; the proportion of Welsh-speakers having fallen from 28.9

per cent in 1951 to 26.0 per cent in 1961. In their study of language patterns based on the 1961 census Emrys Jones and Ieuan Griffiths noted the maintenance of the 'sharp division between Welsh Wales and English Wales', and suggested that 'little can be added to what has previously been said [by Williams, 1937 and Thomas, 1956] about the Anglicized area of Wales'. They concluded, 'The distribution emphasizes that there is a predominantly Welsh Wales, fairly sharply divided from a highly Anglicized area, and yielding territorially only reluctantly to the peripheral advances of the latter' (Jones and Griffiths, 1963, 195). That said, they also noted that rural depopulation had greatly reduced the actual numbers speaking Welsh in the heartland and that consequently territorial resistance should not be mistaken for linguistic strength. Perhaps they should also have stressed the clear development of the fault lines within Welsh Wales; the fractures along which the incipient breakdown of that core was already apparent.

Recognizing perhaps that the future of the language was critically poised on a cusp of change, a whole series of movements, inquiries and initiatives were launched during the following decades. Concern about the health of the language had of course been voiced throughout the first half of the twentieth century, but it was during the 1960s that major efforts were made to strengthen its position. Most notable were developments in the field of education (Williams, Jac L., 1973). Since many of these built on earlier programmes, a brief historical digression is appropriate.

The Welsh Department of the Board of Education was set up in 1907, and in 1927, recognizing the importance of the language issue, a departmental committee published its widely cited report entitled Welsh in Education and Life. In similar fashion, a quarter of a century later, the Central Advisory Panel (Wales) completed its Report on the Place of Welsh and English in the Schools of Wales (1953). It took a firm stance as to the relationship between language and Welsh ethnic identity.

> We cannot support the view that the culture and the ways of life of Wales have no relationship to the language, or that it is quite possible for the non-Welsh-speaking child to partake of the tradition, and the culture of Wales, without a knowledge of the language. There is a close relationship between our language and our culture; the one cannot fully or even adequately be understood without the knowledge of the other. . . '. (Welsh Department, Ministry of Education, 1953, 16)

A firm recommendation followed, that –

> having due regard to the varied abilities and aptitudes of pupils, and of the varied linguistic patterns in which at present they live, the children of the whole of Wales, including Monmouthshire, should be taught Welsh and English according to their ability to profit from such instruction. (p.17)

In 1939 the first Welsh-medium primary school had been established at Aberystwyth, although it was independent and did not come under the Local Education Authority until

1951. The first local authority school was actually opened at Llanelli in 1947. In 1952 the Welsh-medium Schools Movement (Mudiad Ysgolion Cymraeg) was established, and by the time of the 1953 Report there were in addition single schools in Caernarfonshire, Denbighshire, Cardiff and Swansea, and four in Glamorgan and five in Flint. Almost a thousand pupils attended these schools, and such was the demand that further expansion was carefully considered. Thus, in 1956 the Flintshire Education Authority established the first Welsh-medium secondary school, Ysgol Glan Clwyd at Rhyl. A second followed in 1961, and in 1962 Glamorgan set up their first Welsh-language secondary school at Rhydfelin.

It might be added that the first primary school at Aberystwyth owed its founding to the enthusiasm of Sir Ifan ap Owen Edwards. Earlier he had made an equally significant contribution to the promotion of the Welsh language amongst the young in the establishment of Urdd Gobaith Cymru (The Welsh League of Youth) in 1922. Its membership eventually rose to some 50,000 and, as Dafydd Glyn Jones wrote of it –

> All in all, Yr Urdd's. . . history constitutes an impressive feat in combining idealism, enthusiasm, and ambition with careful planning and skilled manipulation of resources. Of all the different branches of the Welsh language movement today [1972], it must be accounted the one most immediately successful. (Jones, D. G., 1973, 288)

But perhaps most significant of all from the viewpoint of the development of the language was the determination of parents, especially in urban areas of south Wales, to set up Welsh-medium nursery schools. The movement began in 1949 in Maesteg with the creation of Welsh-medium pre-school groups (Cylchoedd Meithrin). Similar groups quickly followed in Cardiff and Barry. By 1970 there were some sixty *ysgolion meithrin* and at the 1971 Eisteddfod at Bangor an organization was set up to promote their growth. Mudiad Ysgolion Meithrin Cymraeg (The Welsh-medium Nursery Schools Movement) has been in recent times one of the most influential sustainers of the language (see below).

These developments embraced the full spectrum of education from nursery school to university and college, and even included provision for Welsh-medium adult education. Together they constituted a combined attempt to restore a key language domain – one that had been all but lost at the turn of the century.

Other developments during the 1960s focused attention on the status of the language in Wales. Thus, in 1963 the Council for Wales and Monmouthshire published its *Report on the Welsh Language Today* (Council for Wales and Monmouthshire, 1963). It was primarily a 'state-of-affairs' report and its conclusions were modest. Even so, its wide review of the use of Welsh in most of the domains of living included discussions on government and administration, working life, leisure, religious worship and education. Recognizing the urgency of the situation, Cymdeithas yr Iaith began to take a more dominant and radical role. Its campaigns, though never specified in such a manner, amounted to a succession of attempts to restore Welsh fully to all the domains of Welsh life. The first was the comparatively minor one of road signs (Tudor, 1989), but subsequently the more central themes of the law, bureaucracy (official forms), administration and government were approached.

As was demonstrated earlier, the major effect of the Act of Union of 1536 had not been universally to proscribe Welsh but to banish it from all official use in law, government and administration. To use modern jargon, the language was marginalized. Over the years efforts were made to change that condition (Lewis, R. 1973; Rees, I. B., 1973). The Welsh Courts Act of 1942 allowed anyone who could demonstrate disadvantage to use Welsh, although the decision remained with the Court not with the individual. As a result of agitation, however, the Hughes-Parry Committee was set up in 1963 'to clarify the status of the Welsh language' and its report – *Legal Status of the Welsh Language* – was published in 1965 (HMSO, 1965). The consequence was the Welsh Language Act of 1967 which effectively gave the unrestricted right to use Welsh in the courts, although practice was to prove rather different (Lewis, R. 1973).

The feeling that little had been accomplished by the 1967 Act led to the establishment of The Council for the Welsh Language and the preparation of yet another report, *A Future for the Welsh Language*. In that report it was stated categorically that

> We find the concept of 'equal validity' totally inadequate to the needs of the Welsh language today. Nor do we share the Hughes-Parry concept of bilingualism. To us, bilingualism means that throughout Wales every individual should be enabled and encouraged to achieve sufficient facility in both Welsh and English to choose which of the two languages to use on all occasions and for all purposes in Wales. (The Council for the Welsh Language, 1978)

This describes the system usually known as the 'personality principle' by which any person can use one of two, or indeed more, official languages according to choice at any time. Not all of the report's recommendations were acted upon, but it helped to maintain the momentum of debate.

In reviewing the efforts that have been made to help revitalize the language, one further domain requires reference – the media. The Anglicizing impact of television became a major concern (Rees, 1973) and the demand for a Welsh-medium channel grew rapidly throughout the 1970s. The report *A Future for the Welsh Language* highlighted the urgency for such a provision. In its seventh recommendation it stated that

> . . . in the case of Welsh, the most powerful external influence affecting the home is broadcasting. . . We recommend that the government in the very near future, should make funds available to enable the fourth television channel in Wales to be established and maintained. (The Council for the Welsh Language, 1978, 21/2 and 63/4)

Not without drama, S4C (Sianel Pedwar Cymru – the Welsh Fourth Channel) was established in 1982. In considering the media it is also important to mention the support for the written word through the rapid expansion of Welsh publications. The roles of the Welsh

Arts Council, and particularly of the Welsh Books Council, which was established in 1962, have been particularly important in this regard.

Despite all of these efforts to promote the use and status of the language, the situation deteriorated alarmingly during the 1960s and early 1970s. In no small measure this was due to powerful demographic forces. Out-migration, especially of the young, continued apace while in-migration of non-Welsh-speakers overwhelmed many communities within the heart of *Y Fro Gymraeg*. The problem of rural depopulation was long-standing of course and characterized all except the most prosperous parts during the first half of the century. Inevitably, depopulation was a prime concern of academic analysis and government action. The reasons for the long phase of population loss are well known and were well treated in the Beacham Report – *Depopulation in Mid Wales* (HMSO, 1964). They need not be repeated here. What is more problematic, however, is the impact that depopulation had on language; such matters were not part of the remit of the group that produced the 1964 report. A simple loss of population on its own, unless it is language specific, will not alter the proportion of Welsh-speakers in individual communities. That this was the case is attested by the stability exhibited in the spatial patterns for 1961. It will have an effect, however, on the absolute numbers of speakers. Furthermore, the process would disturb age structures, since those moving out were primarily the younger and more active sections of the population. The consequences of rural depopulation were therefore not necessarily a fall in the proportion of Welsh-speakers or an apparent diminution in the Welshness of *Y Fro Gymraeg*, but a very considerable loss in language vitality.

Such a loss became all the more significant with the demographic changes which followed after 1961. Without entering into statistical detail it can be noted that most districts of rural Wales between 1961 and 1981 showed a gain in population, largely due to a turnaround in migratory flows. For the Welsh language in-migration became a major issue. The reasons for this reversal have again been widely analysed, and are commonly associated with the processes of rural retreating and counter-urbanization (Champion, 1987). The majority of incomers were those who felt moved to reject urban lifestyles and who, with capital often gained from the sale of metropolitan property, were able to settle in more congenial environments, both physical and social. As was widely publicized, the inflow also included other social groupings (hippies, drop-outs, artists etc.); less wealthy perhaps, but also in search of alternative life-styles. The critical point as far as the well-being of the language was concerned was that this in-migration was of a sufficient order even to hide the continued out-migration of young people from the rural heartland.

In contrast, during this critical twenty-year period, there were signs of a continuing resurgence of the language in selected parts of urban and sub-urban south-east Wales and in parts of the borderland. This development is of major consequence and will be developed more fully later; it can partly be explained by the emergence of the transactional city during the latter part of the twentieth century.

The twentieth century has inverted the old profile of the division of labour. In the past most workers were occupied in the production of goods, that is in agriculture, mining and manufacture. . . A small minority of white-collar workers served in the management of public and private affairs. . . In our century this minority has grown enormously while the other sectors of the labour force have shrunk. (Gottmann, 1987)

It is a process which is often referred to as de-industrialization. But it also impacts upon agriculture where the demand for labour, too, is limited. The city is now essentially a centre of transactions of all varieties, a manipulator of information flows based on electronic information technology. The main protagonists are the administrators, the bankers and financiers, and those working in marketing, advertising and the media.

These trends, which have been common throughout the western world, have had a significant effect in Wales. De-industrialization, symbolized by the elimination of the coal-mining industry, has led to significant population loss. This in turn meant the undermining of coalfield communities where if Welsh was no longer central it was still a distinctive element, especially in those areas of the anthracite coalfield where the largest numbers of Welsh- speakers in Wales were to be found. Likewise, agriculture was not able to sustain employment and it too saw a diminution of the labour-force. In complete contrast, the administrative towns, such as Carmarthen or Mold have experienced increases, if not within their boundaries then within their commuting areas. But the epitome of the transactional city in Wales is Cardiff (Aitchison and Carter, 1987). Characteristically, the proposed development at Cardiff Bay symbolizes the role and functions of the transactional city – administration, banking and finance, leisure, together with gentrification in the provision of housing. But in Wales, with the new attention to language which this and the previous chapter have traced, facility in Welsh, if not an essential, is certainly seen as a great advantage; less so in the business world, more so in administration, and especially so in media where S4C obviously must demand proficiency. There has, therefore, been a clear migratory flow from rural Wales to the administrative towns, that is of Welsh-speakers from *Y Fro Gymraeg* to the early Anglicized and urban areas of Wales. There they have demanded Welsh-medium schools for their children and the right to use Welsh in daily life – that is for the operation of the personality principle.

Since an appreciation of these critical regional shifts is essential to an understanding of the contemporary situation, as depicted in the 1991 census, it is appropriate at this juncture to present a series of map distributions for the period 1961–1981. They summarize the main findings of a previous study undertaken by Aitchison and Carter (1985).

Relative Dominance of Welsh-speakers

Figures 4.1, 4.2 and 4.3 record the percentages of the total population (aged 3 and over) who claimed to be able to speak Welsh for the years 1961, 1971 and 1981. Each of the maps is based on a consistent set of class intervals and can therefore be directly compared and contrasted. Together they offer a generalized visual impression of the changing strength or concentration of the language at community level. Again it must be stressed that these maps reveal nothing of the change in actual numbers but are indicative of the

47

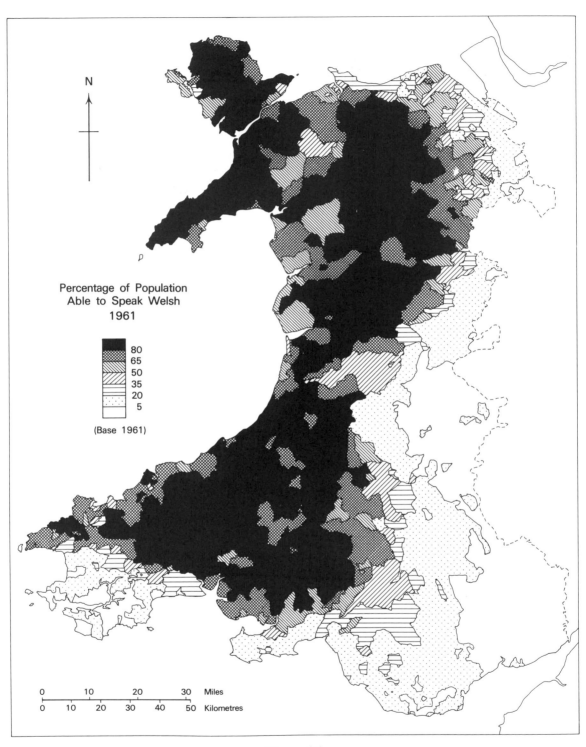

Percentage of Population
Able to Speak Welsh
1961

80
65
50
35
20
5

(Base 1961)

| 0 | 10 | 20 | 30 | Miles |
| 0 | 10 | 20 | 30 | 40 | 50 | Kilometres |

Figure 4.1

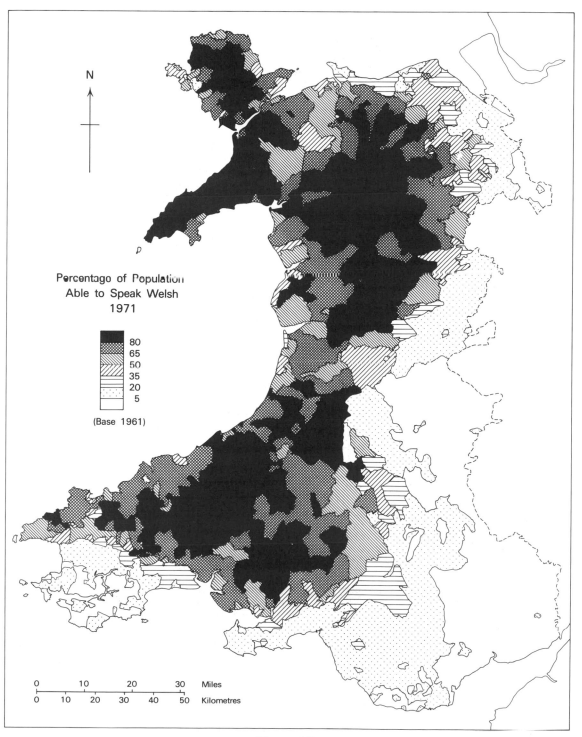

Figure 4.2

relative status of the language within the regions concerned. Changes in the proportion of Welsh-speakers at county level (pre-1974 counties) for the same period are recorded in Table 4.1.

Table 4.1
Percentage of population able to speak Welsh, 1961–1981

County (pre-1974)	1961	1971	1981
Anglesey	75.5	65.7	61.0
Breconshire	28.1	22.9	19.3
Caernarfonshire	68.3	62.0	59.7
Cardiganshire	74.8	67.6	63.2
Carmarthenshire	75.1	66.5	60.0
Denbighshire	34.8	28.1	24.2
Flintshire	19.0	14.7	13.5
Glamorgan	17.2	11.8	10.0
Merioneth	75.9	73.5	68.2
Monmouthshire	3.4	2.1	2.7
Montgomeryshire	32.3	28.1	24.0
Pembrokeshire	24.4	20.7	18.1
Radnorshire	4.5	3.7	5.0
Wales	**26.0**	**20.8**	**18.9**

It has been noted earlier that in their study of the language situation in 1961, Jones and Griffiths wrote of a resilient 'Welsh Wales' yielding only slowly to forces of Anglicization. The extent and strength of that heartland is well delineated in Figure 4.1. As Tables 4.2 and 4.3 show, in 279 of the 993 communities Welsh-speakers accounted for over 80 per cent of the total population over the age of three. Furthermore, in terms of area these same communities claimed a notable 37 per cent of the national territory. Welsh was the dominant language (percentages in excess of 50) in 454 communities. Together, these covered almost 57 per cent of Wales. Such was the continued hold of the language in 1961 that it was still possible to traverse Wales from Llanfairynghornwy at the north-western extremity of Anglesey to Kidwelly on the Carmarthen coast of south Wales, without having to leave a community (at that time parish) in which over 80 per cent of the population was able to speak Welsh. Perhaps more surprisingly, it would almost have been possible to do the same in a west–east direction – from the tip of the Llŷn peninsula to very near the English border at the south-eastern limit of the parish of Llanrhaeadr-ym-Mochnant in the former county of Montgomeryshire.

There were inevitably temporary local anomalies which disturbed the continuity of the pattern. The largest of them was caused by the influx of workers into Trawsfynydd during the construction of the nuclear power plant, whilst, less spectacularly, a similar impact was made by the building of the hydro-electric project at Cwm Rheidol, near Aberystwyth. But, taking these exceptional developments into account, the overall picture is one of a compact and relatively extensive heartland in which the Welsh language was pre-eminent. Having said that, however, it is necessary to recall that the geography of the situation, as it expressed itself in 1961, was but a phase in the longstanding and persistent retreat of the language which was traced in chapter 3. Already the indications of fault lines within the core were apparent and they were to become the major features of change in the succeeding decade.

Table 4.2
Percentage of population able to speak Welsh
by numbers of communities

Classes	1961	1971	1981
Under 5	194	224	209
5–20	239	243	278
21–35	59	51	66
36–50	47	60	76
51–65	61	76	114
66–80	114	148	184
Over 80	279	191	66

Table 4.3
Percentage of population able to speak Welsh by areas of communities

	1961		1971		1981	
	Area (km²)	%	Area (km²)	%	Area (km²)	%
Under 5	2973	14.3	3353	17.0	3139	15.2
5–20	3846	18.5	3870	18.6	4615	22.2
21–35	1055	5.1	1028	5.0	1552	7.5
36–50	1145	5.5	1228	5.9	1700	8.2
51–65	1276	6.2	1828	8.8	2557	12.2
66–80	2830	13.6	3579	17.3	5193	24.9
Over 80	7637	36.8	5694	27.4	2006	9.7

A comparison of Figures 4.1 and 4.2 suggests that the Welsh-speaking heartland had by 1971 been quite heavily eroded. As Table 4.2 reveals, the number of communities with over 80 per cent of their population able to speak Welsh had fallen to 191. That is, 88 of the 279 communities of 1961 had fallen below that level. Those communities covered only 27.4 per cent of the national territory compared with the 36.8 per cent in 1961. The contraction manifested itself most dramatically in the apparent break up of the previously compact core. Although there were indications at earlier dates, it was clear by 1971 that five separate Welsh-speaking nuclei had devolved from the once discrete and consolidated *Bro Gymraeg* (Bowen and Carter, 1975). The main fracture lines had been Afon Menai, the line across Snowdonia from Conwy to Porthmadog, the Severn Valley and the break that divided rural and industrial Dyfed. These will be discussed below when the 1981 pattern is analysed.

Although it was in evidence before 1961, the Anglicization of coastal margins in the former counties of Anglesey, Caernarfonshire, Denbighshire, Merioneth and Cardiganshire, as well as of the lowland valleys penetrating the interior, was particularly intense throughout the 1961–71 decade. But whereas the interior fault lines continued to deepen, the line of the eastern frontier remained fairly stable, with quite sharp gradients dividing the Welsh and English-speaking areas. One surprising exception was the 'landsker' zone in Pembrokeshire, a divide which had remained virtually unmoved for many centuries, but which now showed clear signs of retreat (see below).

Given the fact that the fall in absolute numbers of Welsh-speakers between 1971 and 1981 was of a much lower order than that recorded during the previous decade, the differences in the pattern of percentages for the two censal years as shown in Figures 4.2 and 4.3 respectively, was both unexpected and disturbing in its extent. The statistics in Tables 4.2 and 4.3 vividly demonstrate that the period 1971 to 1981 witnessed a major collapse in the number of communities with over 80 per cent of their population able to speak Welsh. In 1981 only 66 communities were in that category compared with 279 in 1961. Together they accounted for a mere 9.7 per cent of the total area of Wales in contrast to the 36.8 per cent of 1961. Whilst that development was of major significance it must be tempered by the fact that in 364 communities, covering 47 per cent of the land surface of Wales, Welsh-speakers were still in the majority.

In terms of their spatial expression, the patterns of change suggested an exacerbation of the movements which had been apparent in the previous decade. But there were some new developments which can be enumerated.

(i) In Anglesey the growth of tourism and the popularity of the region for retirement contributed significantly to the Anglicization of the coastal communities, with a subsequent encroachment on the strong central Welsh-speaking core area. Between 1961 and 1981 such communities as Llanbadrig, Llaniestyn Rural, Llaneilian, Llanfair Mathafan Eithaf, Pentraeth, Llanddona, Llandegfan, Llangeinwen and Llanynghedl, all experienced major reductions in the proportions able to speak Welsh, that is percentage differences between the two dates of over 20 per cent.

(ii) Anglicizing influences continued to operate throughout the period along the coast of north Wales. This was effectively a continuing westward ripple effect, associated once again with retirement and tourism, although locally modified by suburbanization. During the twenty years the proportion speaking Welsh in Conwy fell from 42.0 per cent to 30.4 per cent, that of Llanfairfechan from 58.1 per cent to 42.0 per cent and that of Llanllechid from 87.0 per cent to 67.8 per cent.

(iii) In Snowdonia, the wedge of Anglicization which entered the massif from the lower Conwy valley, and which was observed as early as 1931, both widened and deepened. The

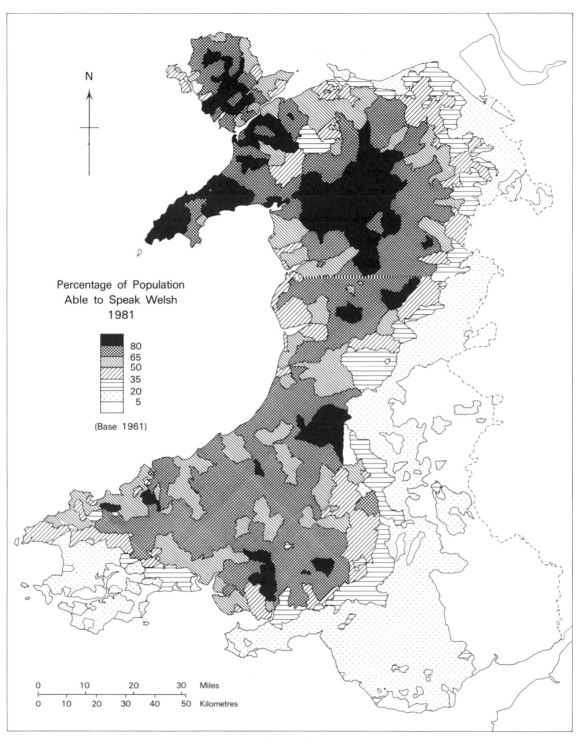

Percentage of Population
Able to Speak Welsh
1981

80
65
50
35
20
5

(Base 1961)

0   10   20   30   Miles
0   10   20   30   40   50   Kilometres

Figure 4.3

percentage of Welsh-speakers in the community of Capel Curig, for instance, fell very sharply from 45.7 per cent to 28.6.

(iv) The proportions of Welsh-speakers in many communities along the coast of west Wales, from Harlech in the north to the St David's Peninsula in the south, fell very considerably. Whereas in 1961 quite extensive areas returned percentages in excess of 80, by 1981 such was the pace of relative decline that not a single community on the coast sustained percentages of that order of magnitude. So significant were the inroads into the Welsh-speaking cores of Meirionydd and Ceredigion that it became possible to consider this coastal fringe as giving rise to a new frontier of language dilution, parallelling the long-standing divide within the border counties to the east. The possibility of two frontiers inexorably moving towards each other and pinching out the interior core, constituted a major threat to the traditional language heartland.

(v) At various points along the eastern edge of the Welsh-speaking heartland there were clear signs of a softening of the once sharp language gradients. Whilst the map distributions alone suggest a quickening of the pace of change between 1971 and 1981, it is evident that the process extended over the whole of the twenty years under review. This can be illustrated by considering a line of communities across the eastern edge of Mynydd Hiraethog. Thus in the west, within *Y Fro Gymraeg*, the percentage of Welsh-speakers in Cerrig-y-drudion fell from 90.8 in 1961 to 89.6 in 1971 and 86.8 in 1981, a discernible but minor retreat. However, further to the east the three decadal percentages for Clocaenog were 88.9, 75.0, and 61.4; for Llanynys 79.4, 72.8 and 64.2; for Efenechtyd 74.4, 69.8 and 57.6. The sharper falls in the later decade are quite evident and indicate a retreat of that frontier which in 1961 had been described as strongly resistant to Anglicization.

(vi) In central Wales, the wedge of Anglicization which followed the upper sections of the Severn had clearly gained in strength, penetrating almost to the coast. With the declining community percentages in the hinterland of Aberystwyth, the Welsh-speaking areas of Meirionydd and Dyfed, which were effectively continuous in 1951, were being prised further apart.

(vii) Writing of the 'Landsker' in 1972, John stated that 'the present-day divide is a cultural feature of surprising tenacity; it is quite as discernible, and only a little less strong, than the divide of four centuries ago. In the landsker we have a unique cultural heritage' (John, 1972, 7). The evidence of the map distributions, however, would suggest that in terms of the Welsh-speaking proportions the landsker was suffering the fate of the other language bulwarks, and was retreating. Thus, if a band of nine communities is taken across Pembrokeshire from Llandeloy in the west through Puncheston and Castleblythe to Llandissilio in the east, then it will be seen that in 1961 all nine, apart from Llandeloy (77.2) and Letterston (71.0) recorded percentages of Welsh-speakers over 80. In 1981 none of them did; and only one was over 75. Llandeloy had fallen to 43.7 per cent from 77.0, and Letterston to 55.2 from 71 per cent.

(viii) Along the southern and eastern edges of the main Welsh-speaking core area of Dyfed similar patterns of relative decline were apparent. In the parish of Llanelli Rural, for example, the percentage of Welsh-speakers fell from 69.2 to 46.7 in 1981. Similar figures could be cited for other communities skirting the fringes of this region with its large population of Welsh-speakers.

This part of the analysis has considered changes in percentages of Welsh-speakers. Since the relationship between relative and absolute values is not necessarily direct or positive, consideration now needs to be given to regional variations in the actual number of Welsh-speakers.

Absolute Change in Numbers of Welsh-Speakers

In 1961 the total number of Welsh-speakers enumerated in Wales stood at 656,002. During the decade which followed that figure fell to 542,425. As Figure 4.4 vividly demonstrates, losses were greatest in the industrial valleys of south Wales. By 1971 Rhondda had 11,938 fewer Welsh-speakers, Merthyr Tydfil 5,224 and Aberdare 5,039. Further west the Welsh-speaking population of Swansea declined by 6,517 and of Llanelli by 5,035. These are in part due to direct population loss as major restructuring programmes for the coal, iron and steel and tinplate industries had an enormous impact upon the well-being of the region and forced many to leave it in search of work. This pattern of industrial decline and out-migration repeated itself in the coal-mining areas of north-east Wales. Between 1961 and 1971 the community of Rhosllanerchrugog, for instance, lost 1,778 Welsh-speakers. Communities bordering the Dee estuary recorded similar, if less dramatic decreases. There were also falls in settlements along the north Wales coast, Bangor recorded a decrease of 1,328 and Llandudno of 530.

One point which needs to be considered when reviewing the fall in numbers in areas such as the old industrial centres and the retirement settlements along the coasts, is the age structure of the population. The high ratio of elderly naturally leads to greater declines.

Absolute decreases in other rural areas were inevitably less spectacular, although Denbigh fell by 924 and Ffestiniog by 669. While small, such decreases were of considerable significance to the communities concerned. The explanation here, too, lies in the frailty of the local economies. The problems faced by small family farms, especially in the upland and marginal areas, and of small businesses in general, were critical. They contributed to a steady depopulation of the countryside and a concomitant loss of Welsh-speakers.

Whilst the overwhelming impression is one of decline, it is interesting to note that between 1961 and 1971 a number of communities actually recorded increases in their Welsh- speaking populations. As Figure 4.5 demonstrates, however, absolute increases were confined to communities in the more anglicized parts of Wales, for example suburban Cardiff, the Alyn and Deeside District of north-east Wales and South Pembroke. Within the main Welsh-speaking areas, isolated but notable increases were recorded by such communities as Llangefni, Llanfairpwll and Amlwch on the island of Anglesey,

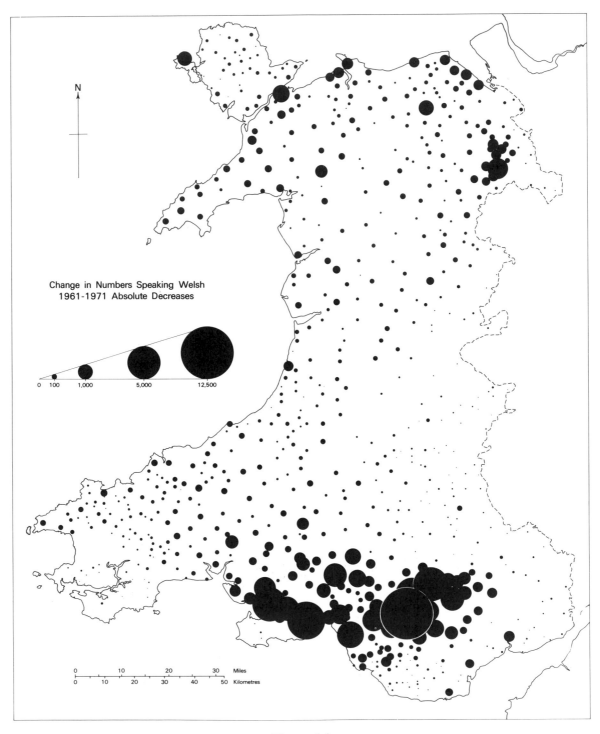

Change in Numbers Speaking Welsh
1961-1971 Absolute Decreases

0   100   1,000   5,000   12,500

Figure 4.4

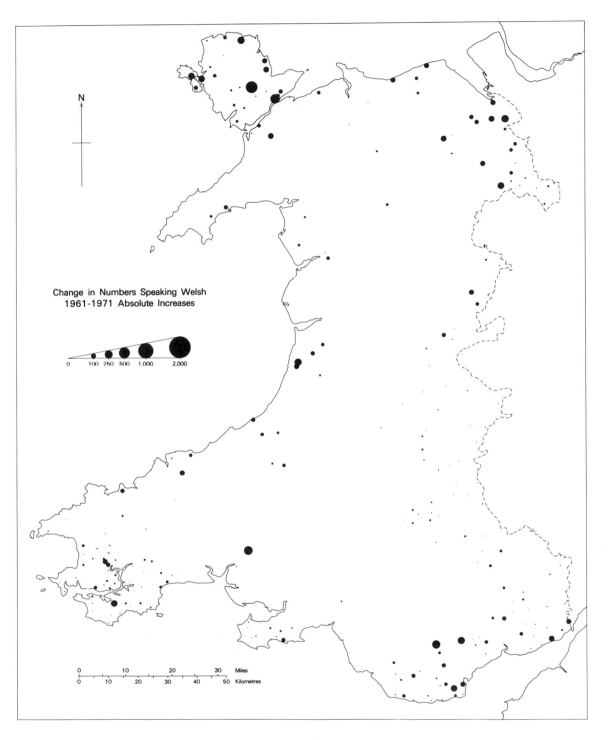

Change in Numbers Speaking Welsh
1961-1971 Absolute Increases

0   100 250 500 1,000   2,000

0   10   20   30   Miles
0   10   20   30   40   50   Kilometres

Figure 4.5

Llangunnor (Llangynnwr) to the east of Carmarthen, and Upper Vaenor near Aberystwyth. It is difficult to offer a general explanation, but certainly most of these were in suburban locations.

Between 1971 and 1981 the total population of Welsh-speakers enumerated in Wales continued to decline, but at a much reduced rate. With a fall of 6.3 per cent for the decade, the total in 1981 was 508,207 (using the 1971 population base). Figure 4.6 shows the pattern of decline at the community level. In broad terms it repeats that described for the period 1961–71. The old industrial heartlands of south and north-east Wales once again account for the bulk of the national loss, although the numbers are reduced. Throughout rural Wales, falls in the numbers of Welsh-speakers are also noticeably lighter. Interestingly, relatively high losses were recorded for the two university towns of Aberystwyth (-775) and Bangor (-951). This anomaly is partly explained by the timing of the censuses in relation to student vacations, but it certainly does not explain the whole situation.

Again, many communities showed increases (Figure 4.7), the dominant growth points being Cardiff with its surrounding communities in the District of Taff-Ely and the southern parts of the Rhymney Valley, as well as the Newport, Cwmbran and Pontypool axis. Significant increases were also in evidence in north-east Wales around Mold and Connah's Quay, and on Anglesey. During the seventies, a number of these areas benefited from the expansion of job opportunities in national and local government, in various administrative and commercial organizations, and in the mass media and entertainment sector, especially television. For employment in many of those, the ability to speak Welsh was either essential or highly advantageous. The establishment of bilingual secondary education also undoubtedly contributed to a resurgence of interest, a point which will be taken up later as it becomes particularly apparent in the next decade. The immediate import of these areas of increase is that they highlight a very significant revival of the language beyond the traditional heartland and point the way to crucial changes in process.

Percentage Rates of Change in Numbers of Welsh-speakers

Between 1961 and 1971 the number of Welsh-speakers fell by a massive 17.3 per cent, from a total of 656,002 to 542,425. Table 4.4 shows that decreases in excess of 10 per cent were recorded in all but three of the pre-1974 counties. The pace of decline slackened somewhat between 1971 and 1981, but the Welsh-speaking population still contracted by 6.3 per cent. Notable proportionate increases were, however, returned in the areas of the former counties of Radnor and Monmouth, whilst Anglesey and Flint experienced more marginal gains. Elsewhere, Welsh-speaking populations declined, and most dramatically in the old county of Glamorgan

Figures 4.8, 4.9 and 4.10 focus on patterns of relative change in the number of Welsh-speakers for the intercensal periods 1961–71 and 1971–81. Figures 4.8 and 4.9 show percentage change, whilst Figure 4.10 categorizes communities according to trends during

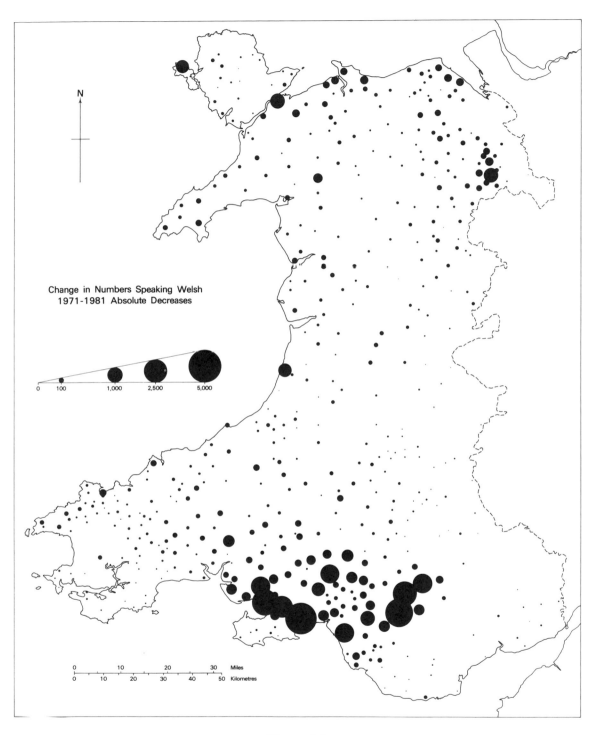

Change in Numbers Speaking Welsh
1971-1981 Absolute Decreases

0   100   1,000   2,500   5,000

0   10   20   30   Miles
0   10   20   30   40   50   Kilometres

Figure 4.6

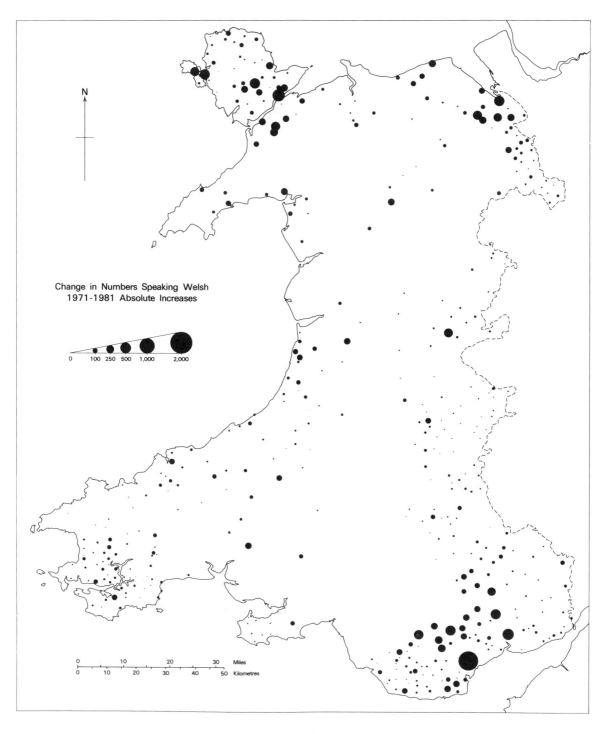

Figure 4.7

Table 4.4
Percentage change in numbers able to speak Welsh

County (pre-1974)	1961–1971	1971–1981
Anglesey	-0.03	5.98
Breconshire	-21.18	-10.30
Caernarfonshire	-8.49	-2.28
Cardiganshire	-7.10	-1.79
Carmarthenshire	-14.15	-10.27
Denbighshire	-14.45	-6.99
Flintshire	-10.22	-4.48
Glamorgan	-14.96	-29.79
Merioneth	-10.37	-4.77
Monmouthshire	-35.85	27.78
Montgomeryshire	-14.80	-3.74
Pembrokeshire	-10.74	-2.98
Radnorshire	-17.09	58.17
Wales	**-17.31**	**-6.34**

the two intercensal periods. To aid comparison, the scales adopted for Figures 4.8 and 4.9 have been standardized. The frequency of communities within each of the eight categories used in these maps is given in Table 4.5. It will be noted that the total number of communities referred to in this tabulation varies for the two periods concerned. This is because it is not possible to calculate rates of change for those communities with no Welsh-speakers in either of the base years.

Table 4.5
Change in numbers able to speak Welsh:
numbers of communities by percentage classes

Percentage Classes	1961–1971		1971–1981	
	Numbers of Communities	% Total	Number of Communities	% Total
Over 50	78	8.1	107	11.5
21 to 50	55	5.7	82	8.8
0 to 20	101	10.4	210	22.6
0 to -10	165	17.0	198	21.2
-11 to -20	213	22.0	135	14.5
-21 to -30	154	15.9	89	9.6
-31 to -50	111	11.5	69	7.4
Over -50	91	9.4	41	4.4
Total	**968**	**100.0**	**931**	**100.0**

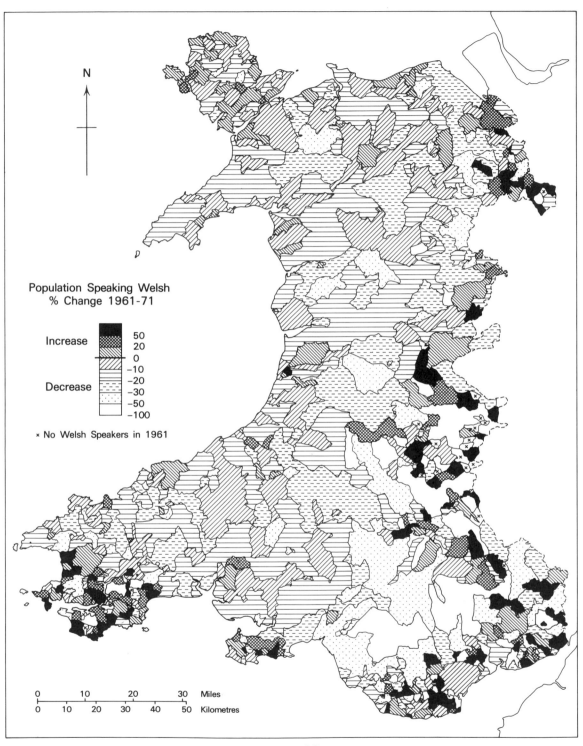

Figure 4.8

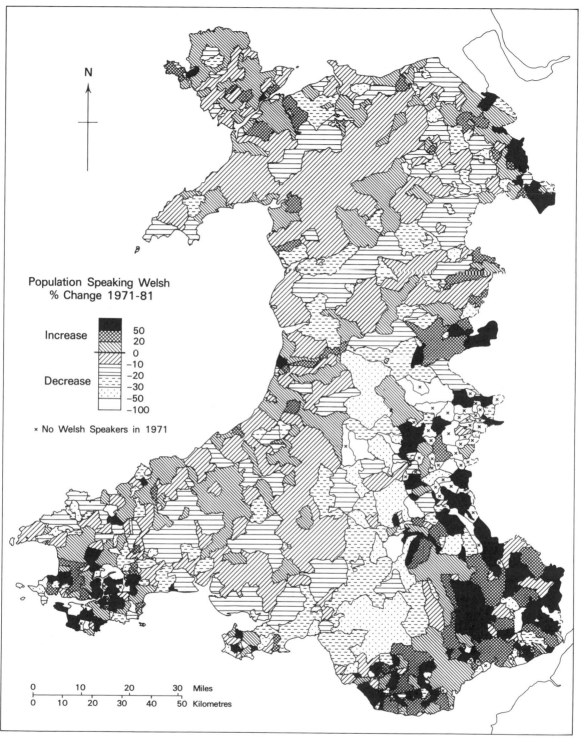

Figure 4.9

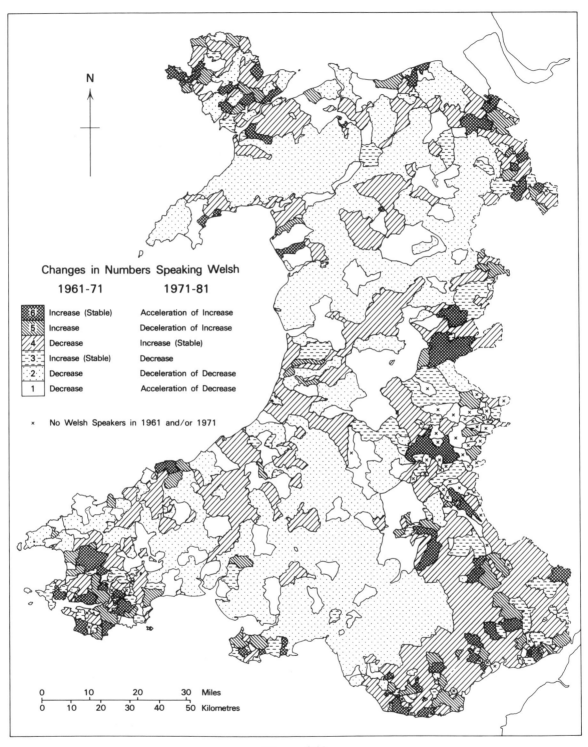

Figure 4.10

Table 4.5 shows that between 1971 and 1981 a total of 399 communities recorded increases in their number of Welsh-speakers, and that in 107 of them the increases were in excess of 50 per cent. Admittedly, many of the high increases were returned by communities with rather low Welsh-speaking populations, for example in the borderlands and Pembrokeshire. Nevertheless, that represented a distinct improvement on the situation between 1961 and 1971. Then, only 234 communities showed a positive rate of change.

The data also indicate that, whilst the number of communities recording negative rates of up to -10 per cent increased, 165 in 1961–71 as against 198 in 1971–81, there was a substantial fall in the number with the greater relative decreases. Thus, 91 communities experienced a loss of Welsh-speakers in excess of 50 per cent for 1961–71 as against only 41 for the following decade.

In order to present a clearer picture of the changes detailed in Figure 4.8 and 4.9, an attempt has been made to draw together both sets of information in a single classification of communities. Figure 4.10 presents a six-fold categorization of communities according to the direction and rates of change over the two periods. The nature of each of the six categories is described in the key to the map, and Table 4.6 lists the associated number of communities, together with mean rates of change for the two periods.

Table 4.6
Numbers of Welsh-speakers: change categories
1961–1971 and 1971–1981

Categories	Number of Communities	Mean % 1961–71	Mean % 1971–81
1	143	-15.6	-28.1
2	277	-24.1	-12.6
3	87	58.2	-34.5
4	260	-24.1	40.1
5	80	100.5	24.3
6	82	19.5	55.4

(See Figure 4.10 for category definitions)

Category 1 is made up of those communities (143 in all) where the number of Welsh-speakers declined continuously over the two decades, but where the pace of decline increased between 1971 and 1981. These are the major problem regions for the language. It is evident from Figure 4.10 that they are scattered throughout Wales. Significant clusters covered substantial areas of land in western and central Montgomery, and in central parts of Brecknock. The large number of communities belonging to this category in central parts of Dyfed, and their highly fragmented distribution, underlines the complexity and often localized character of language decline in these most vulnerable areas. Even so, it is possible to associate them in very general terms with the main areas of loss as identified in the earlier section on trends in differences. Certainly there seems to be a link with the main frontier of retreat; hence the representation in Montgomery and Brecknock. Between 1961 and 1971 the average rate of decline was -15.6 per cent, whilst for 1971–81 it was -28.1.

Category 2 contains the greatest number of communities (277) and extends over a large part of south-west Wales (excluding South Pembrokeshire), Gwynedd and Clwyd. The majority of communities within the main Welsh-speaking area belong to this category. It is defined by continuous decrease, but one which slackened during the second of the two decades. Average statistics suggest a decline of 24.1 per cent, followed by one of 12.6 per cent. The fact that categories 1 and 2 dominantly characterize both urban and rural regions of Welsh-speaking Wales is clearly indicative of the crucial problems which those areas faced in terms of language survival.

Category 3 includes those communities that experienced an increase or stability in numbers of Welsh-speakers between 1961 and 1971, but a decline in the decade that followed. This applies to a scattering of communities, mainly located in borderland regions. With the small numbers involved it is difficult to assess the precise significance of this sharp, and seemingly anomalous, reversal of fortunes.

In contrast, comfort could be derived from the presence within the heartland of a sizable number of communities which registered increases in their Welsh-speaking population between 1971 and 1981, after having experienced losses in the previous decade. These communities make up category 4. They are seen to be concentrated in more westerly locations, especially in Ceredigion and Gwynedd, but are patchy in nature. The majority, however, are situated in south-east Wales. The most extensive grouping includes communities in the Vale of Glamorgan, southern parts of Mid Glamorgan, Gwent and south-east Brecknock. Developments in these areas have already been noted as a distinctive feature of the 1971–81 decade. Their potential significance for the future of the Welsh language is further emphasized by the presence within the areas they cover of many communities which fall into categories 5 and 6. As Table 4.6 indicates these categories define areas where there was continuous growth in the numbers of people able to speak Welsh. Away from the south-east, there were marked concentrations of this type in South Pembrokeshire, in Anglesey and in north-east Wales where Mold seemed to be the focus.

Conclusion

This chapter has attempted to highlight the major forces that impressed on the geography of the Welsh language during what must be seen as a particularly critical period in its history. By the beginning of the 1960s the language appeared to be entering a deep spiral of decline from which it would not be able to extricate itself. Although major new initiatives were launched to help retrieve matters, the situation deteriorated markedly between 1961 and 1971. However, despite continuing pressures in the decade that followed, signs of a slackening in the pace of decline were in evidence as the efforts to improve the status and use of the language began to assert themselves. That said, it is clear that conditions in the main rural heartlands were still a cause for concern, while the full significance of the seemingly positive developments taking place in certain urban areas needed to be treated circumspectly. It is to these matters, and their implications for the language during the 1980s, that the discussion now turns.

CHAPTER 5

The Welsh Language in the 1980s: A Decade of Mixed Blessings

During the 1980s many of the positive and negative forces that have been alluded to previously continued to impact on the Welsh language. There were, however, new developments of considerable significance for the long-term future of the language at national and local levels. Added to these were countervailing trends of an international order which also figured prominently. It is not possible here to elaborate in detail on these initiatives and tendencies, the more limited intention is to provide a very broad overview and then to capture some of the main changes taking place during the decade through two detailed case studies. The one examines language patterns in an archetypal Welsh-speaking rural area (centred on the settlements of Tregaron and Llangeitho in Ceredigion), the other explores recent developments in Cardiff and its environs.

To set the context for these case studies, it is appropriate to make a number of broad observations on some general changes of relevance to the condition of the language in rural and urban regions of Wales. Firstly, there is the demographic situation. Table 5.1 records absolute and relative trends in the resident populations of rural districts between 1981 and 1991. The statistics show that during the 1980s numbers increased in all areas, although with significant variations between districts. Thus, growth rates in excess of 8 per cent were recorded for Colwyn (13.4%), Ceredigion (10.4%), Radnor (9.7%), South Pembrokeshire (8.8%) and Montgomeryshire (8.1%), while in Brecknock, Preseli Pembrokeshire and Ynys Môn they were less than 2 per cent. It is evident from Table 5.1 that the increase in population totals was mainly due to in-migration, although in some instances natural increases also contributed to the expansion. The process of counter-urbanization that began in the previous decade continued to assert itself, albeit at a reduced pace. The origins of those moving into rural Wales are difficult to ascertain for the entire period, but it is likely that significant percentages emanated from England. The situation in Ceredigion demonstrates the point. Here, for the year preceding the 1981 census, there was an inflow of 5,598; of these 1,357 (24%) came from England, with nearly 42 per cent of these being from the South-East. This movement, which affected many parts of rural Wales, clearly maintained pressure on the language, and not only at its geographical margins, but at its very heart. The situation was further exacerbated by the fact that the out-migration of young, and often well qualified, people from the rural heartland still continued in the 1980s, hidden beneath the net migrational increase.

Table 5.1
Rural Wales: population change, 1981–1991

Districts	1	2	3	4	5	6
Colwyn	47283	53622	6339	13.4	-6.9	20.3
Glyndwr	38947	40855	1908	5.0	-2.1	7.1
Carmarthen	50839	53920	3081	6.1	-2.4	8.4
Ceredigion	55353	61109	5756	10.4	-2.3	12.7
Dinefwr	36606	37798	1192	3.3	-3.2	6.5
Preseli Pembrokeshire	67688	68638	950	1.4	1.6	-0.2
South Pembrokeshire	37593	40896	3303	8.8	0.7	8.1
Aberconwy	49621	51262	1641	3.3	-5.4	8.7
Arfon	50295	51461	1166	2.3	1.6	0.7
Dwyfor	25409	26419	1010	4.0	-5.2	9.2
Meirionnydd	30458	31963	1505	4.9	-3.3	8.2
Ynys Môn	66496	67371	875	1.3	1.9	-0.5
Brecknock	39536	40206	670	1.7	-2.2	3.9
Montgomeryshire	47649	51527	3878	8.1	-0.3	8.4
Radnor	20940	22982	2042	9.7	-1.9	11.7

KEY

1. Resident Population 1981   *4. % Population Change*
2. Resident Population 1991 (1981 base)   *5. % Natural Change*
3. Absolute Population Change   *6. % Migrational Change*

(Source: OPCS County Monitors)

Also reinforced during the 1980s was the process of de-industrialization and the dominance of Cardiff as a transactional city. Both of these trends had impacts on the geography of the language. The loss of population from the mining valleys of South Wales negatively affected numbers of Welsh-speakers, most especially in the anthracite coalfield where large concentrations of speakers were to be found. However, contrary trends were operative in many small administrative towns and in their associated sub-urban areas. Here, growth in residential populations was often accompanied by an increase in numbers of Welsh-speakers (e.g., Mold and Carmarthen). Most dramatic of all, however, was the increase in employment opportunities for Welsh- speakers in the Cardiff region. Positions in administration and the media continued to attract upwardly-mobile people to the area, many of whom came from *Y Fro Gymraeg*. Here, in this long-Anglicized urban setting, they demanded even further provision of Welsh-medium schools for their children, and a Welsh-speaking social environment steadily established itself.

While these various demographic developments had mixed impacts on the language, some negative and some positive, more planned initiatives to support its development continued to flourish. Formally, the most noteworthy was the creation in 1988 by the Secretary of State of yet another body with special commitment to the needs of the language – The Welsh Language Board. Its remit was to advise on language matters in general, and to promote wider use of Welsh in both public and private spheres. The Board outlined a strategy for the period 1989–94 which recognized the need to 'improve the infrastructure of the Welsh language' and ensure 'ways in which the two languages in Wales can live side by side' (Welsh Language Board, 1989, 5). Although the Board placed emphasis on the notion of a 'community of languages' and 'bilingualism', this 'does not mean that everything has to be done bilingually in every part of the country. Political, social and resource constraints are going to have a very strong influence on the pattern of services that will be provided when the strategy is interpreted at local level' (Welsh Language Board, 1989, 5). A further notion to be given emphasis was that of 'normalization', a concept similar to that of the personality principle. The term, which is widely used in the European arena of lesser-used languages, is construed by the Welsh Language Board to mean ensuring that 'it is possible, convenient and normal for everyone, in every situation where a public service is provided, to choose which language he or she wishes to use' (Welsh Language Board, 1989, 5). But since the Board itself only published its strategy in 1989 its impact on Welsh language figures in the 1991 census must be minimal. Accordingly, further discussion of such matters is left to the conclusion.

As has been noted, it is not possible or appropriate in this geolinguistic study to enter into a detailed review of the many initiatives that were launched in support of the language during the 1980s. A wide-ranging and accessible summary of these is available in the report Language Strategy 1991–2001 drawn up and published by the National Language Forum (1991), itself a body with an extensive representation, and characteristic of the determination to advance the language. In this strategic report there are sections on the statutory status of the language, of its employment in education, local and central government, health and social services, the economy and industry, publishing and the media, the churches, societies and voluntary bodies, as well as the relationship to housing and migration. Of these, two of the most important are education and the media – they warrant further comment for they figure in the case studies that follow.

During the 1980s considerable advances were made in Welsh-medium education at all levels. The Welsh-medium Nursery Schools Movement continued to expand and by 1990 there were 553 nursery groups and nearly 345 'mother and child' groups throughout Wales. Together they catered for nearly 13,000 children. Significantly, 60 per cent of these came from non-Welsh-speaking homes. During this period there was also a steady expansion in the number of Welsh-medium primary schools, most notably in Mid Glamorgan and South Glamorgan. That said, statistics for 1988 suggested that throughout Wales just 13 per cent of primary school children spoke Welsh fluently. A further 74 per cent had no Welsh whatsoever. As far as secondary education is concerned the picture was very variable. The fact that in 1988 over 80 per cent of pupils received Welsh lessons in their first year of secondary school is significant; less so is the fact that for the fourth year this figure stood at 28 per cent.

Although it does not influence the results of the 1991 census, it is appropriate at this point to note that in 1988 the Education Reform Act came into force. This Act is of immense importance to the future of the language since it ensures that all children aged between 5 and 16 will be introduced to the language at school. This is because the Act accords Welsh the status of a core subject in Welsh-medium schools and a foundation subject in all others.

Advances in the provision of Welsh-medium courses in colleges of further education were not as impressive as in the primary and secondary sectors, although there was a notable increase in opportunities for certain vocational courses (e.g., business, catering). Progress in higher education was also exceedingly slow, at least within the constituent University Colleges of Wales. It was only in 1979 for instance that a Board was established to oversee the promotion of teaching through the medium of Welsh. Greater support for the language came from the training colleges, in particular those at Bangor and Carmarthen. It has to be said, however, that within the University of Wales problems of finance have certainly hampered developments in the field of Welsh-medium education.

The second area of support for the language worthy of special reference is that of the media. It is now widely recognized that the establishment of Radio Cymru in 1979 was a most significant development and contributed greatly to the promotion of the language. However, it was the long-awaited decision to set up Sianel 4 Cymru (Broadcasting Act 1981) that was of pivotal import. Its significance cannot be exaggerated. Not only does it offer instruction in the language, an instruction which was once provided by chapel and Sunday school; more crucially, it serves as a base on which to build sentiment. It is a revealing feature of post-modern Wales that an element of the mass media has to be substituted for the chapel, and the synthetic communities of soap operas have replaced community in the real world. But in the decade of the 1980s the gradual evolution of S4C into such a role has been manifest, especially as it takes steps to adapt its language to everyday usage.

While an appreciation of these various specific developments are central to an understanding of the forces at work within the language domain, others of a more global and contradictory nature entrenched themselves during the 1980s. If universal movements of modern times have been generally threatening to the language, the nature of the post-modern world can be considered as very different. Post-modernism can be defined as the ultimate in eclecticism, and if that is inadequate as a definition it at least gives some indication of what has characterized the last decade. The western world has been marked by the decline of large scale certainties and a break down into movements and ideas which are far more ragged and less dominated by overriding notions. Perhaps the rise of what has been called the 'single-issue fanatic', one who devotes total effort to a single issue which is not necessarily related to any standard or coherent philosophy, is the clearest symptom. Animal rights, anti-smoking or environmental issues of all sorts are examples.

All this does have implications for language. It could well be argued, for instance, that Cymdeithas yr Iaith was one of the first of the single-issue organizations. And as the old universalist philosophies of the right and left, of both Thatcherite Conservatism and pure socialism, both declined into a form of pragmatism, so Cymdeithas yr Iaith was able to exert more influence. It succeeded in placing the language firmly in the centre of the political agenda in a way that it could not have hoped to when monolithic parties and their philosophies dominated the political scene.

More important than the changes in political philosophy, at least in everyday terms, has been its concomitant in terms of political reality. It is perhaps an exaggeration to write of the collapse of the nation state, though not of the questioning as to its relevance as a late medieval structure at the end of the twentieth century when new associations are being sought, both at higher and lower levels of territorial identity. Many contemporary states came into being during the early modern period through conquest or dynastic means, many before the association of ethnic identity with political entity was common. Now the constituent parts of these aggregations are asserting their own rights to separate or devolved government. At the heart of the matter is an appropriate territorial hierarchy, where the old nation state no longer takes unquestioning priority and where each level from federal union to state and the components of the state, to region and to locality, has its proper and appropriate function. It is a difficult process to enable, especially where ethnic groups are intermixed or have mingled over a period of time. It is even more difficult where ethnic groups claim the same territory. Many of these problems were created by the application by western colonialism of the principle of the nation state in Africa and Asia, regardless of tribal areas or traditional territorial systems. But the general contemporary theme is quite clear: these so-called regional conflicts have replaced the old imperial confrontations. The present is not witnessing 'the end of history' but a different post-modern history. Internal colonization as a concept has been long out of fashion, but it might be possible to argue that the post-war decolonization of the external pieces of empire is now being followed by internal decolonization.

If Wales is considered in relation to these tendencies then superficially there are considerable advantages for the language. A clear continent-wide trend to devolution and regionalism must seem to the good; a Europe of the 'Regions' greatly appealing. Certainly its representation in such organizations as The European Bureau for Lesser-Used Languages is indicative of a European movement to reinvigorate the minority languages. It is also symbolic of post-modern trends. But an automatic assumption that in a separate or devolved Wales language would be greatly advantaged needs to be questioned, as a reference back to the statement by Saunders Lewis thirty years ago and quoted in the introduction to chapter 4 would suggest, and as some of the discussion in chapter 1 indicated. Nevertheless, the operation of these trends during the 1980s has undoubtedly made the language issue widely significant. No longer were large-scale movements entirely inimical to the language: a turnaround in values and ideologies that could prove to be of considerable importance in the long term.

Having traced broad trends and movements of relevance to an understanding of the process of language change, it is apposite at this point to explore the situation, as it manifested itself at the local level during the 1980s. Two case studies are considered; together they capture the extremes of change that characterized the period. The studies themselves are based on behavioural and attitudinal surveys of schoolchildren and their parents, firstly in a traditional Welsh-speaking rural community (Aitchison, Carter and Rogers, 1989), and secondly in an urban area experiencing a resurgence of interest in the language (Aitchison and Carter, 1988).

The Tregaron Region

The first locality to be examined (henceforth referred to as the Tregaron region) comprises a set of twelve communities that lie within the catchment area of Ysgol Uwchradd Tregaron (Tregaron Comprehensive School). Questionnaire surveys of pupils at this school and of their parents generated data on family backgrounds and use of the Welsh language in differing domains.

The demographic characteristics of the region are displayed in Table 5.2 . They confirm that the area experienced a significant loss of population between 1961 and 1971, but then, in common with other parts of rural Wales, witnessed the impact of a turnaround during the decade that followed. For the two inter-censal periods however it is noteworthy that numbers of Welsh-speakers continued to decline, although the pace slackened considerably between 1971 and 1981. In 1981 nearly 77 per cent of the resident population were able to speak Welsh. This is a high figure and would appear to suggest that all was well with the language in the region. In fact this was far from being the case, for in 1961 nearly 92 per cent of the local population were Welsh-speakers. It is evident that heavy in-migration had significantly transformed social and linguistic structures in the area. The situation varied from community to community, but the severity of the change in the community of Llangeitho was most remarkable, for there the percentage of Welsh-speakers fell from 82.9 in 1971 to just 54.2 in 1981.

Questionnaires for the language survey were completed by 301 pupils (88% of the school population). Virtually all of these were Welsh-speakers, and most (78%) had attended Welsh-medium primary schools. Some 48 per cent of the Welsh-speaking pupils had learned the language at home, the remainder had received their first introduction to it at school. Whilst these figures appear encouraging, the situation is more critically poised when reference is made to the relative standing of Welsh vis-à-vis English, and to the use that is made of the language in different domains. Just over half the pupils indicated that they were able to speak Welsh either better than English (34%), or at least as well as English (17%). For the rest, English was their favoured language. This relatively even split can partly be explained by reference to the home backgrounds of the pupils, for although 47 per cent came from households where both parents were able to speak Welsh, a notable 38 per cent indicated that neither parent could speak the language. The remaining 15 per cent (including some single-parent families) stated that just one parent could speak Welsh. Given this situation it is hardly surprising that a high proportion of pupils (41.7%) claimed that they never spoke Welsh at home (Table 5.3).

That said, Welsh is still seen to be the dominant medium of communication in homes where both parents were able to speak the language, although it is noteworthy that nearly 19 per cent of such homes made little or no use of Welsh.

Tables 5.4, 5.5 and 5.6 record the use of Welsh relative to English in the school playground and outside school, both absolutely and in relation to parents' language abilities.

73

Table 5.2
The Tregaron area: change in population over the age of three.
Welsh-speaking population and proportion born in Wales

Community	Population % Change		Welsh-speaking % Change		Welsh-speaking	Welsh-born
	61–71	71–81	61–71	71–81	1981	1981
Blaenpennal	7.8	1.7	-4.9	-2.6	79.5	73.7
Caron is Clawdd	-6.4	4.6	-7.8	-0.4	84.4	82.8
Caron u. Clawdd	-17.7	28.3	-19.5	12.1	80.9	71.4
Gwnnws Issa	-14.1	13.9	-24.0	-1.5	68.1	69.7
Gwynfil	7.1	3.3	-4.5	-1.2	77.4	70.6
Llanbadarn Odwyn	-24.3	29.6	-28.0	14.4	69.1	58.3
Llanddewibrefi	-12.9	6.9	-19.9	-7.4	76.6	72.0
Llangeitho	-4.5	17.9	-13.7	-22.6	54.5	54.2
Lower Lledrod	4.3	40.0	-0.9	21.4	74.3	72.4
Upper Gwnnws	-15.5	-9.3	-13.9	-18.8	85.7	84.8
Upper Lledrod	-18.8	4.8	-26.8	6.7	73.3	68.8
Ysbyty Ystwyth	-19.4	15.1	-25.3	-10.3	67.6	65.8
Tregaron region	**-9.1**	**10.1**	**-14.0**	**-2.4**	**76.7**	**70.4**

Table 5.3
Use of Welsh at home by linguistic status of households

	Number of parents able to speak Welsh		
Percentage speaking Welsh	Both	One	Neither
More than English	75.4	9.3	0.0
Same as English	6.0	11.6	0.0
Only a little	11.2	34.9	15.6
Never	7.4	44.2	84.4

Table 5.4
Use of Welsh in the playground and outside school

Percentage speaking Welsh	Playground	Outside school
More than English	27.0	29.1
Same as English	17.8	14.2
Only a little	17.1	17.6
Never	38.1	39.1

Table 5.5
Use of Welsh in playground by linguistic character of household

	Number of parents able to speak Welsh		
Percentage speaking Welsh	Both	One	Neither
More than English	54.1	11.6	0.0
Same as English	27.8	18.6	5.5
Only a little	2.8	27.9	18.1
Never	5.3	41.9	76.4

Table 5.6
Use of Welsh outside school by linguistic character of household

	Number of parents able to speak Welsh		
Percentage speaking Welsh	Both	One	Neither
More than English	58.1	11.9	0.0
Same as English	25.0	11.9	1.8
Only a little	11.8	28.6	20.7
Never	5.1	47.6	77.5

Given the significant number of pupils who had moved into the area from outside Wales (see below), the figures indicate a higher level of social use than might perhaps have been expected. Even so, just over a third of all pupils claimed that they never communicated with their friends in Welsh. But it is also evident that pupils from dominantly Welsh homes maintained a relatively strong hold on the language, despite the obvious pressures which might have obliged them to make more extensive use of English. In both domains nearly 85 per cent of pupils from Welsh-speaking homes used the language at least as frequently as English, with the majority actually speaking it to a greater extent. Those pupils from non-Welsh speaking backgrounds inevitably used Welsh to a much smaller degree, but even there a quarter did say that they made some use of the language beyond the classroom.

The pupils of Tregaron school professed a high degree of literacy, with over 70 per cent stating that they had little difficulty in reading and writing Welsh. But a high proportion admitted to reading only a very limited amount of literature written in Welsh outside school. This again was clearly related to the language of the parents; an impressive 68.9 per cent of pupils from Welsh-speaking homes read books and newspapers in Welsh either 'often' or 'quite frequently'. Recognizing the important role that television can play in the promotion of the language, it is significant that 79.4 per cent of those questioned watched Welsh language television 'often' or 'quite frequently', though the percentage fell to 25.6

where only one parent was Welsh speaking. Radio was by no means as popular, and only 41.9 per cent from households where both parents spoke Welsh listened 'often' or 'quite frequently', with 58 per cent returning 'hardly ever' or 'never'.

An important cultural feature of the Tregaron area is the access that pupils have to clubs and societies where Welsh is spoken regularly. That these groups play a key role in helping to promote and consolidate the language was confirmed by the high proportion (45%) of pupils who actually attended meetings and events organized by such bodies as the Urdd, YFC (Young Farmers Clubs) and others. More significantly, 70 per cent of pupils from Welsh-speaking homes participated in such societies.

Another finding of considerable interest was the attitude of children to the 'value' of Welsh in finding employment. Where both parents spoke Welsh, 99.2 per cent thought that the ability to speak Welsh was an advantage in seeking work, but even more surprisingly 93.5 per cent of those where neither parent spoke Welsh were of the same opinion. Such responses are not unrelated to the fact that just over two-thirds confirmed a wish to live and work in Wales after leaving school.

Finally, given the centrality of the in-migration issue to the changes taking place in the region, it is of relevance to note that only 62 per cent of the pupils were actually born in Wales; of those the great majority (90%) were born in Ceredigion. Birthplaces of the remainder included the South-East (21%), the West Midlands (6%) and the North-West (5%). Equally revealing was the fact that many of the school children had moved into the area only recently, 28 per cent having done so within the previous five years.

Having ascertained the behaviour and attitudes of pupils to the Welsh language it was appropriate to deepen the analysis through a survey of parents. Just over 200 responded to the questionnaire, and of these some 40 per cent were born outside Wales. Intermarriage between locals and incomers was of a relatively low order. Thus, out of the 95 respondents born in Ceredigion, 67 had married someone from the same area. In fact, there were only 7 marriage partners born in England. Certainly at this stage 'mixed' marriages do not seem to be a problem for language maintenance and the key issue is the general impact of 'pure' English families on the standing and use of the language. However, the limited degree of intermarriage is probably a consequence of the recency of the in-migratory movement. In that respect there were significant findings, for a goodly proportion of those born outside the area claimed to speak Welsh. Of the 160 respondents and spouses born outside Wales, nearly 44 per cent indicated that they could speak Welsh. Put in another way, of the 283 parents able to speak Welsh nearly a quarter had been born outside Wales. It is also notable that whilst the majority of Welsh-speaking parents came from homes where both their parents were able to speak Welsh, a significantly high proportion, some 24 per cent, came from homes where neither parent was able to speak the language. The latter were predominantly incomers who first learned to speak Welsh by attending beginners' courses. Nearly 13 per cent of the Welsh-speakers had been able to speak the language for less than five years; another 6 per cent had been speaking it for between 5 and 10 years.

Table 5.7
Parents use of Welsh in different domains

Respondents' use of Welsh:	Percentages speaking Welsh		
	In the home	At work	Socially
More often than English	59.1	53.7	59.9
About the same as English	5.4	19.4	10.6
Hardly ever	22.8	16.4	19.7
Never	12.7	10.5	9.9

The data presented in Table 5.7 suggest that for the parents Welsh was the dominant medium of communication in all language domains, with over 50 per cent stating that they used Welsh more often than English. Thus a strong core of adults had maintained a positive commitment to the language in their everyday activities. On the other hand, about 30 per cent of Welsh-speakers made very little use of the language, though a significant percentage of these were Welsh learners. Again, nearly 70 per cent claimed that they could both read and write Welsh. Some 60 per cent stated that they watched Welsh-language television regularly or fairly often. In contrast to the schoolchildren, a high number also listened to radio in Welsh, just over 30 per cent regularly and a further 19 per cent often.

The parents, like their children, saw real economic advantage in being able to speak Welsh. Almost 66 per cent of the respondents thought it a 'great' help and 32.3 per cent 'some' help in securing employment. Even more encouraging from the point of view of the language was the fact that 72.5 per cent of the respondents and 72.2 per cent of their spouses considered it important that their children should be able to speak Welsh. The fact that over 70 per cent of respondents hoped to stay in the region at least for the next ten years, boded well for increased cultural integration.

It is evident from the two sets of surveys that the Tregaron region experienced a major social and linguistic re-structuring during the 1980s. A typically Welsh environment was radically transformed as a result of the steady flow of in-migrants from urban parts of England. This influx, coupled with the continuing out-migration of young Welsh-speakers, had a major impact on the absolute and relative standing of the Welsh language in the area. Although in-migration could clearly be viewed as a major threat to the language at this time, it has to be noted that a substantial number of incomers had made efforts to learn Welsh, and, furthermore, were happy to see their children become part of the Welsh-speaking community. In general the investigation suggested that the Tregaron region was poised at a critical threshold. Cultural and linguistic continuity clearly depends on the relation between the strength of the host population and numbers of incomers. There is a level where in-migrants can be integrated, and indeed fall under pressure to integrate, and where they can add vitality to a community. But there is also a level where, because of the relatively high numbers, absorption does not take place, nor is it seen as necessary. There is

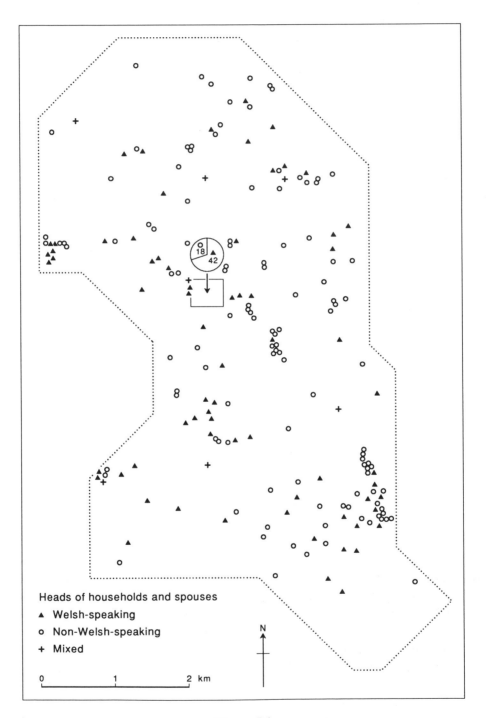

Figure 5.1

a 'tipping point' where the domains of language use become restricted, the supporting cultural environment becomes attenuated and Anglicization intensifies. In the mid-1980s that point had not quite been reached in the Tregaron region. The Welshness of the area was sufficiently robust, and the educational system both for children and adults, sufficiently supportive, to have prevented it. Even so, the area appeared to be moving close to a situation where irreversible trends could assert themselves.

This possibility was reinforced by a detailed study of the language of households in two communities within the hinterland of Tregaron (Aitchison, Baptiste and Edwards, 1990). Relating to the period 1970–90 and based on an analysis of electoral registers, the investigation revealed quite dramatic changes. Figure 5.1 shows the location of Welsh-and non-Welsh-speaking households in the area in 1990 and captures the enormity of the language shifts which had taken place over a twenty year period. In 1971 a very high proportion of the households in the area (some 84%) were able to speak Welsh. Evidence gained in the field surveys suggested that this had fallen to nearly 40 per cent by the late 1980s. The swarm of English-speaking homes in what was only a short time ago a community dominated by a population of isolated and dispersed farmsteads, where traditional Welsh values and the language were safeguarded, is graphically representative of the changes which have taken place in many other parts of rural Wales. The dwindling number of children from Welsh-speaking homes attending the local schools, and the size of congregations in the chapels, are but two manifestations of a deep-seated cultural transformation; some would say malaise.

The Cardiff Region

The nature of urban growth in the post-industrial period and its implications for the Welsh language have already been broadly summarized. The intention of the study undertaken in the Cardiff region was to examine in more detail the significance of these developments for an area deemed to be experiencing a 'quiet' language revolution (Aitchison and Carter, 1987). Adopting the same questionnaires as those used in the Tregaron region a series of school communities was investigated. Given their crucial significance to language developments in the region special consideration was given to Welsh-medium schools.

The promotion of Welsh-medium teaching in Cardiff and its environs is not a recent phenomenon. As early as 1897, for instance, the Cardiff School Board passed a resolution in favour of teaching the language. In the same year a survey of over 6,000 parents yielded a massive 81 per cent return in support of Welsh-language provision within the schools of the city. In 1907, another survey of parents generated less positive responses, but even so it showed some 40 per cent in favour of their children being taught Welsh. Be that as it may, it was only in 1949 that the first Welsh-medium primary school was established – the Ninian Park School. That was some ten years after a special committee had been set up to consider Welsh-language provision. In its deliberations, the committee was somewhat belatedly responding to the highly influential 1927 Report to the Board of Education entitled *Welsh in Education and Life* (see chapter 4).

In 1952 the City of Cardiff Education Committee published a comprehensive report on the teaching of Welsh in the city's schools. It placed pupils into three language classes: those for whom Welsh was a mother tongue (5%); those who could understand Welsh (10–15%); and those unable to speak Welsh (80–85%). The report also noted the increasing number of pupils taking Welsh as a subject, the proportion rising from 60 per cent in 1940 to 72 per cent in 1952, a period during which Welsh was not compulsory. At the same time, growth in the number of children attending the Ninian Park primary school necessitated a move to a new site at Highfields in Llandaf, with the school changing its name to Ysgol Gymraeg Bryntaf. It was to prepare children for entry into that new school that the first *ysgol feithrin* in Cardiff was established in the vestry of Capel Heol y Crwys in May 1951.

In March 1961 an application was made to the Education Authority for a Welsh primary school to serve Rhiwbeina and Whitchurch. The application was refused, but a Welsh-medium unit was opened at Ysgol Llanishen Fach in 1965. Meanwhile, 1962 saw the creation of Ysgol Gyfun Rhydfelen, the first Welsh-medium secondary school in the then county of Glamorgan.

In 1972 yet another Welsh language survey was launched, with parents of six to ten year olds being asked to indicate whether or not they wished their children to learn Welsh. The results identified nine schools where there appeared to be significant support for a bilingual stream – Birchgrove, Llanedeyrn, Baden Powell, Moorland, Eglwys Newydd, Springwood, Hawthorn, Ton yr Ywen and Lansdowne. Accommodation problems created difficulties for certain of these schools, but bilingual units were eventually established at the infant and junior schools in Rhiwbeina, Ton yr Ywen, Cefn Onn, Lansdowne and Eglwys Newydd. Following further growth in numbers, and difficulties experienced in the transport of pupils to and from school, there were again calls for a restructuring of Ysgol Gymraeg Bryntaf. It was expected that the school would be split into three separate schools, but in the end the decision was taken to move the site to the Parade, a step which many considered detrimental to the development of Welsh-medium education.

In 1976 the Director of Education for the newly constituted county of South Glamorgan recommended that three Welsh-medium primary schools be established: Coed Glas (Llanishen) in 1977, Eglwys Wen (Whitchurch) and Peter Lea School (Fairwater) in 1978. With the change in the county structure, increasing pressure developed for South Glamorgan to provide its own secondary education through the medium of Welsh rather then relying on Ysgol Rhydfelen, now in Mid Glamorgan. At the time some 100 pupils were receiving secondary education either at Rhydfelen or at Llanhari, also in Mid Glamorgan and established in 1974. Indeed, with growing demand Mid Glamorgan Education Authority made it known that it would not be able to accept pupils from South Glamorgan after 1978. As a result, though not without some local dissent, Ysgol Gyfun Gymraeg Glantaf was opened in 1978 with 100 pupils.

At the time of the survey, and following the closure of Bryntaf in 1983, there were within the City of Cardiff five Welsh-medium primary schools – Ysgol Melin Gryffydd at

Whitchurch (Yr Eglwys Newydd), Ysgol Coed y Gof at Pentrebane (Pentrebaen), Ysgol Bro Eirwg at Llanrhymni, Ysgol y Wern at Llanishen (Llanisien) and Ysgol Gymraeg Radnor Road in Canton (Cantwn). Within the main settlements of Cardiff's commuting hinterland there were other Welsh-medium primary schools, as well as the two important secondary schools at Rhydfelen and Llanhari.

This review of the growth of Welsh-medium education in Cardiff affirms the response made to a growing demand from parents and reflects the pattern of in-migration into Cardiff from the Welsh-speaking heartland. To evaluate the situation in more detail a sample of five primary and four secondary schools was selected for study. From a preliminary survey of all headmasters and headmistresses it was evident that Welsh-medium schools claimed virtually all the young Welsh-speaking population in the region. A highly polarized and asymmetric structure prevailed, with the vast majority of schools having no fluent Welsh-speakers at all. It appeared from this introductory survey that little basis existed in the education system for a movement to a bilingual city. This being the case, it was pertinent to ask to what extent the Welsh-medium schools, as products of the economic and social changes in progress in Wales, provided more than a tenuous hope for the future in a context which is regarded by many as quite crucial. It was to shed some light on that question that a series of surveys were undertaken.

For the surveys three separate questionnaires were administered. One was directed to pupils in the fifth and sixth forms of four secondary schools; the second was completed by parents of the secondary school children; the third was distributed to parents of children attending primary schools. Given that the vast majority of Welsh-speaking children attended Welsh-medium schools, it was to those that the bulk of the questionnaires inevitably had to be directed.

The survey of the four secondary schools yielded a total of 856 responses. For purposes of reference it should be noted that in the tabulations that follow schools 2, 3 and 4 were official Welsh-medium schools; almost all of the pupils in these schools answered the questionnaire in Welsh.

Table 5.8
Cardiff secondary schools: ability to speak Welsh

	Schools			
	1	2	3	4
Percentage able to speak Welsh:				
Better than English	0.6	17.8	10.4	6.0
As well as English	0.7	40.2	36.4	55.0
Not as well as English	23.0	41.5	50.9	39.0
Only a little	75.7	0.4	2.3	0.0

A feature of Table 5.8, which records ability in speaking Welsh, is the relatively high percentages of pupils in all the Welsh-medium schools who stated that they could not speak Welsh as well as they could English. The figure was as high as 51 per cent in school 3. On the other hand some 61 per cent in school 4 indicated that their Welsh was as good as their English. The questionnaire revealed that the great majority of pupils had learned Welsh at school rather than at home, the 'at school' percentages for the four schools being 91.9, 50.2, 75.0 and 86.0 respectively. That was to be expected given the relatively low proportion of homes where both parents were Welsh speaking. As reported by the pupils, the relevant percentages for the four schools were 7.4, 39.2, 23.0 and 10.2. Not surprisingly, this situation affects responses relating to the actual use of Welsh in the home (Table 5.9).

Table 5.9
Cardiff secondary schools: use of Welsh in the home

	Schools			
	1	2	3	4
Percentage speaking Welsh:				
More often than English	1.3	30.4	11.7	6.0
About the same as English	0.7	11.2	9.3	8.6
Only a little	8.7	30.4	31.3	44.2
Never	89.3	27.9	48.0	41.1

Given the limited use of Welsh at home, it is perhaps not surprising that use of the language in the playground and outside the home should be of an equally low order. Thus, 92.6, 23.9, 52.0 and 39.5 per cent of pupils stated that they never used Welsh outside of the school. Similar responses emerged in relation to viewing television and listening to the radio in Welsh, and reading Welsh books. Thus, the 'hardly ever' and 'never' categories for the use of Welsh-language television and radio were 90.2, 43.1, 58.6 and 56.0 and 100, 79.7, 88.0 and 89.2, respectively. The equivalent figures for the four schools for reading books and papers were 94.7, 61.8, 59.8 and 59.2 per cent. Again, the percentages attending clubs and societies where Welsh was regularly spoken were low: 10.7, 32.8, 14.6, 15.3. It is evident from these figures that in this growth area it is difficult for the Welsh language to move out of the domain of the schools for the whole of the economic, social and cultural environment is predominantly Anglicized. Even so, there was a general feeling on the part of pupils that an ability to speak Welsh was an advantage in seeking employment. Only 37.9 per cent thought it of no help at all in the non-Welsh-medium school, while the figures in the Welsh-medium schools were, as might be expected, very low at 6.2, 7.3, and 8.0. Interestingly, the great majority of pupils in the Welsh-medium schools stated that they wished to stay in Wales after leaving school.

The associated survey of parents generated responses from 409 families. The results need not be considered in detail here, but two general observations are worth noting. Firstly, parents' estimates of their own ability to speak Welsh differed from that of their children. It has been mentioned above that the proportion of homes with Welsh-speaking parents was relatively low (based on the returns made by pupils). The responses from the parents themselves, however, yielded a set of proportions that suggested a higher level of competence in the language (Table 5.10). Overall 67 per cent of parents claimed to be able to speak Welsh. Various reasons could be cited to account for this discrepancy, but it is of interest to note that a third of those parents who stated they could speak Welsh actually came from non-Welsh-speaking homes and had made efforts to learn the language (Table 5.11). The second observation is that the use of Welsh by parents was highly circumscribed in the main domains (at work and socially). Here, only between 30 and 50 per cent of Welsh-speakers used the language 'more often than' and 'about the same as' English.

Table 5.10
Ability of parents to speak Welsh by households

Percentage of households:	Schools			
	1	2	3	4
Both parents	10.0	67.7	55.1	29.3
One parent	19.3	25.8	20.2	37.8
Neither parent	70.7	6.5	24.7	32.9

Table 5.11
Ability to speak Welsh: respondents and parents of respondents (Welsh-medium schools only)

Respondents:	Parents of respondents		
	Both	One	Neither
Welsh-speaking	252	97	181
Not Welsh-speaking	15	31	212

The survey of primary schools was limited to five schools, the questionnaires being completed by parents in 181 households. Schools 1, 2, 4, and 5 were Welsh-medium. Table 5.12 shows the recorded ability of parents to speak Welsh.

Table 5.12
Ability of primary school parents to speak Welsh

Percentage of parents:	Schools				
	1	2	3	4	5
Both	28.0	38.0	16.1	62.5	25.7
One	56.0	52.0	12.9	15.6	68.5
Neither	16.0	10.0	71.0	21.9	5.8

The figures reveal a high proportion of households where only one parent was able to speak Welsh, suggesting a rather frail basis for the promotion of the language in the home. This was confirmed by the extent to which Welsh was spoken in the home (Table 5.13).

Table 5.13
Use of Welsh in the home: primary school parents.
Percentages of Welsh-speaking parents

	Schools				
	1	2	3	4	5
More often than English	33.3	43.7	0.0	14.3	39.6
About the same as English	16.7	22.5	0.0	14.3	27.6
Hardly ever	38.9	28.2	30.8	53.6	31.0
Never	11.1	5.6	69.2	17.8	1.7

The results of the survey indicate that the language has only a weak hold on the life of the Welsh-speaking community, with Welsh failing to achieve a dominant position even in the households where the children attended a Welsh-medium school. The same pattern is repeated in the other language domains investigated, with the least use again being in the work place. Since the influence of the chapel has been stressed as one of the preservers of the language and the decline of attendance as a factor in the decline of the language, it is of interest to consider the responses recorded in Table 5.14. The data are unambiguous, and confirm that only small percentages of respondents attend chapels and churches where the services are in Welsh on a regular basis – yet another negative feature of the language situation in the study area. To this can be added the low degree of interest in Welsh-language television and radio.

Table 5.14
Attendance at church/chapel where services are held in Welsh.
Percentage of Welsh-speaking parents

	Schools				
	1	2	3	4	5
Regularly	25.0	23.8	0.0	17.7	29.3
Occasionally	43.2	20.2	7.7	10.7	34.5
Never	31.8	55.9	92.3	71.4	36.2

In sharp contrast, when questions were asked directly about their children the responses from parents were far more encouraging, with high proportions being returned for speaking Welsh 'better' or 'as well as' English, reading material in Welsh, and attending clubs and societies where Welsh was the medium of communication. Percentages ranging between 50 and 60 applied in all of the Welsh-medium schools.

Having briefly summarized the results of these various surveys, it is appropriate to draw a number of conclusions concerning the condition of the language in the Cardiff area. Firstly, it is clear that the use of Welsh is not widely diffused through the region. Welsh-speaking pupils are overwhelmingly concentrated in the Welsh-medium schools. This 'oasis' condition clearly poses problems for the wider promotion of the language.

Whilst the Welsh-medium schools were playing an important role and satisfying a burgeoning demand, the results of the surveys point to underlying and background conditions which are generally not favourable as far as the use of the language is concerned. These relate in the main to the place of the language in domains that lie beyond the classroom – the home, the social environment of both pupils and parents, and their contact with Welsh literature and the media.

Attention has been drawn throughout the analysis to the rather limited use which is made of Welsh in day-to-day communication. This is partly related to the fact that in many households neither, or, at best, only one of the parents were able to speak Welsh. The same could be said in regard to households in their more extended form. To underline this latter point, extended households were classified according to the number of Welsh- speakers. The maximum score was 6 where the two parents and four grandparents spoke Welsh. The results are shown in Table 5.15.

Table 5.15
The Cardiff region surveys: extended households.
Percentage of households

Score	Secondary schools	Primary schools
0	32.5	18.7
1	13.7	19.2
2	13.4	14.3
3	13.7	16.5
4	8.1	15.4
5	5.9	3.3
6	12.7	12.6

There are of course various ways in which the different scores can be obtained, but the overall conclusion is that the home foundation on which the Welsh medium schools are seeking to build is not very deep or strong. That said, the situation could be expected to slowly change as the Welsh-speaking children build their own families: always assuming of course that they stay in the area.

A related weakness, as far as the entrenchment of the language is concerned, is the very limited and seemingly superficial use that was made of Welsh in the playground and in the wider social arena by the pupils of the Welsh-medium schools. Domain limitations also applied to Welsh-speaking parents. There were variations, but generally Welsh was not used to a great extent in the workplace, which would be expected, or in social communication. Equally surprising was the limited interest in Welsh-language television, radio and literature. The reasons offered by way of explanation varied, but often appeared to be mere rationalizations (e.g., comments on the quality of productions and publications).

Somewhat more encouraging findings were related to motivation and future intentions. For there to be a real revival of the language in the Cardiff region there must be a continued build up in the numbers of speakers. The increased provision of Welsh nursery and primary education is fundamental, but equally important is the need to hold young speakers in the region. Responses to questions relating to future intentions indicate that many Welsh-speaking pupils felt that they were likely to seek employment in the local area. Similarly, most parents seemed satisfied with their immediate surroundings. A related and particularly positive development was the large number of parents who had taken steps to learn the language.

An overarching conclusion that can be drawn from these surveys is that as in the Tregaron region, but for different reasons, the language situation in Cardiff is critically poised. There must be doubts as to whether or not there is sufficient momentum for a sustained regeneration of the language. From the predominantly Anglicized environment of the city, and the influences in daily life which are overwhelmingly English, there emerges not even the outline of a strongly identified subculture. Outside very limited domains, indeed outside the school, the use of Welsh at home, at work and at play seems greatly constrained. Without a strong cultural focus, one which was once provided by the chapel, the significant educational efforts are in danger of being seriously dissipated when that special environment is left.

In the region there appeared to be no real wish to have immersion as deeply and as continuously as possible in a Welsh cultural milieu. That particular language subcultures can exist in urban environments is well attested. But the 'urban village' in which such cultural survival takes place needs two attributes – sufficiently large numbers of people and a degree of isolation. Neither of these seems to be apparent in Cardiff.

An interesting and consistent feature from the surveys in both the Tregaron and Cardiff regions is the view that an ability to speak Welsh is a positive attribute when it comes to seeking employment. If this is so, then it represents a complete reversal of the long-standing perception of Welsh as being significant in cultural terms but of no economic value. Whilst such a view may be understandable in Cardiff as a response to the transactional role of the city, it is sadly near the conception of a language as a series of characters for communication, rather than as the matrix of a culture, and it might explain the low ratios for the use of Welsh outside limited domains. Even so, it offers tangible reasons for learning Welsh which did not exist so clearly in the immediate past.

Reflecting on the results of the surveys, Aitchison and Carter (1988, 30) observed that

> At present . . . the Welsh language within Cardiff and its environs is a plant that has grown vigorously but without a deep or extensive root system. The evidence . . . would suggest that, given the pressures in the urban environment at large, it is not yet robust enough to gain a truly meaningful hold and to move out of the 'hot-houses' of the Welsh-medium schools.

This conclusion may be valid, but it cannot be gainsaid that the efforts being made in the area on behalf of the language have been most impressive.

It will be apparent that these detailed local surveys have confirmed many of the conclusions drawn from a consideration of the aggregated data for the period leading up to the 1981 census. Clearly, in the rural areas there have been major problems generated by the forces of counter-urbanization. As has been shown, however, the response has been significant, mainly through advances in the educational system. Endeavours to offer language instruction to adults have also been important, and the number of in-migrants willing to learn Welsh during the 1980s was far from insignificant. In Cardiff the growth of the numbers speaking Welsh has been a distinct feature of the recent history of the language, although the bases and infrastructural context for its fuller and deeper development would appear to be somewhat limited. But before offering a final judgement on these matters and on future prospects for the language, it is necessary to bring the statistical record up-to-date with an analysis of the results of the 1991 census.

CHAPTER 6

The Welsh Language in 1991

In a study of language patterns and trends in rural Wales, Aitchison and Carter (1989) forecast that while the number of Welsh-speakers would continue to decline between 1981 and 1991, the pace of change would be much reduced when compared with previous intercensal periods. It was further proposed that by the year 2001 there would be a turnaround of great historic significance, with numbers of Welsh-speakers actually increasing for the first time since 1911. Given the major efforts that have been made over the past three decades to secure a stronger future for the language the results of the 1991 census have been eagerly awaited.

Unfortunately, as has already been noted (chapter 2), differences in the definition of households, in the form of published tabulations and, most critically, in the boundaries of administrative areas (both wards and communities) make detailed quantitative analyses of patterns of change extremely difficult, if not impossible. Certainly, the standard series of community maps generated for the period 1961–81 (chapter 4) cannot be extended. Be this as it may, in the discussion that follows an attempt is made, wherever possible, to identify what appear to be meaningful trends in language patterns for the period 1981–91. Although it is not feasible to calculate absolute and relative changes and to prepare associated maps, it is in certain instances worth comparing ward distributions for 1981, with those for 1991. It is the ward that constitutes the basic areal unit of study in the main map analyses that follow. Data relating to numbers and percentages of Welsh-speakers for the 908 wards of Wales are included for reference purposes in the Appendix on p. 120.

The Welsh-speaking Population

The 1991 census records a total Welsh-speaking population of 508,098. This represents 18.6 per cent of the total resident population aged three years and over (2,723,623). Table 6.1 shows the distribution of Welsh-speakers at county level. The counties of Dyfed and Gwynedd are seen to be the main strongholds of the language; they account for over half of all Welsh-speakers, with a combined total of 283,411 (55.7%). At the other extreme are the counties of Gwent, Powys and South Glamorgan where resident Welsh-speaking populations are in each case less than 25,000. This regional pattern of absolute figures complements a similar pattern for the percentages of the resident county populations (aged three and over) that are able to speak Welsh. Table 6.1 reaffirms the dominant position of Gwynedd and Dyfed. Here 61.0 and 43.7 per cent of the respective populations are Welsh-speakers. In marked contrast are the counties of Gwent, South Glamorgan and Mid Glamorgan where less than one in 10 people speak the language.

Table 6.1
Population and language statistics (1991)

County	1	2	3
Clwyd	392812	71405	18.2
Dyfed	331528	144998	43.7
Gwent	423794	10339	2.4
Gwynedd	226862	138413	61.0
Mid Glamorgan	511656	43263	8.4
Powys	113335	22871	20.2
South Glamorgan	375857	24541	6.5
West Glamorgan	347779	52268	15.0
Wales	**2723623**	**508098**	**18.6**

KEY
1. Resident population aged 3 years and over
2. Population able to speak Welsh
3. Percentage population able to speak Welsh

Table 6.2 records the same information for the 37 districts of Wales. Five districts have more than 30,000 Welsh-speakers; in order these are Ynys Môn (Anglesey), Arfon, Ceredigion, Llanelli and Carmarthen. It is noteworthy that the districts dominated by the two main cities of Wales – Swansea and Cardiff – also record quite high figures (in excess of 17,000 in both cases). The lowest totals (less than 3,000 Welsh-speakers) are returned by all of the districts in the county of Gwent.

The proportions of the district populations that speak Welsh vary greatly, from a high of 75.4 per cent in Dwyfor to a mere 1.9 per cent in Monmouth. In addition to Dwyfor, six other districts have Welsh-speaking percentages in excess of 50 per cent – Arfon, Dinefwr, Meirionnydd, Ynys Môn, Ceredigion and Carmarthen. Of all the districts, however, 18 actually returned percentages of less than 15. These include the main urban districts of south and north-east Wales, certain rural districts in the borderland, South Pembrokeshire and the Vale of Glamorgan.

A more detailed appreciation of regional patterns is provided in Figures 6.1 and 6.2. Here, the absolute numbers of Welsh-speakers at ward level are recorded, together with associated densities per km². Concerning these maps it is important to emphasize once again that urban regions tend to be depicted by dense clusters of small wards, while in rural regions of Wales (especially in the central uplands) the wards tend to be much more extensive in area. This bias in spatial detail clearly needs to be taken into account in appraising the resultant map distributions.

As is to be expected, the regional pattern of absolute numbers of Welsh-speakers is very similar to that described previously for 1981 (although in this latter instance the base

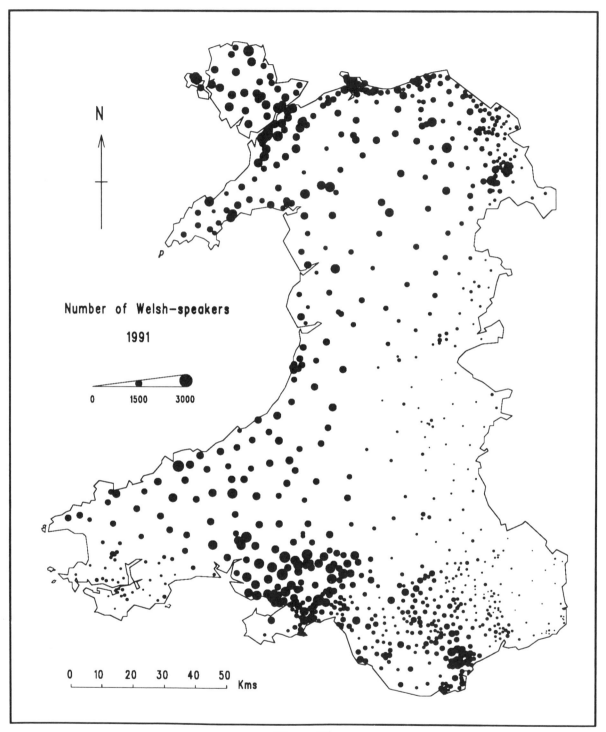

Number of Welsh-speakers

1991

Figure 6.1

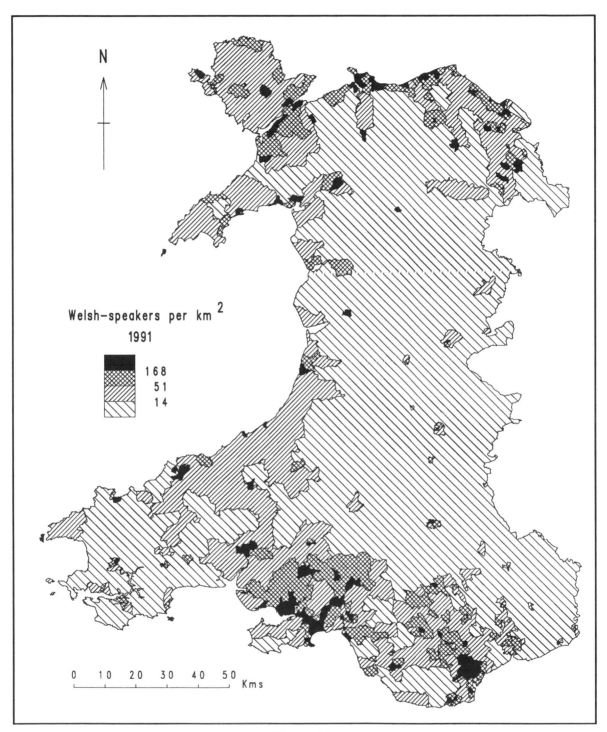

Figure 6.2

reference was communities). Briefly, Figure 6.1 confirms that the majority of Welsh-speakers are located in two main areas. The first, and the most dominant concentration, covers the urban and old industrial heartland of south-west Wales. Wards in and around the towns of Llanelli, Ammanford and Swansea are seen to return particularly high figures (often in excess of 2,000 Welsh-speakers). Examples include Tumble (2,770), Morriston (2,755), Gorslas (2,602), Gwauncaegurwen (2,204), Ystalyfera (2,110) and Pontardawe (2,093). To the east of this core, a dense swarm of wards with relatively small numbers of Welsh-speakers merges into a much stronger cluster in the immediate hinterland of Cardiff.

The second main zone with relatively high concentrations of Welsh-speakers extends along the coast of north Wales, from Caernarfon in the west to Flint in the east. The wards that make up the towns of Caernarfon, Bangor and Conwy–Llandudno have significant numbers of Welsh-speakers. At its eastern end this coastal zone extends inland and takes in the urban areas of Wrexham and Ruabon. Along the coast of west Wales concentrations of Welsh-speakers are to be found in the towns of Holyhead, Pwllheli, Porthmadog, Ffestiniog, Dolgellau, Aberystwyth and Cardigan. Relatively high figures are also associated within selected inland market towns; for example, Carmarthen and Llandeilo in the Vale of Tywi, Denbigh and Rhuthun in the Vale of Clwyd, Llanrwst in the Vale of Conwy, Llandyssul and Lampeter in the Vale of Teifi, and finally Newtown and Welshpool in the Vale of Powys.

Table 6.2
Population and language statistics (1991)

Districts	1	2	3
Alyn and Deeside	70502	6779	9.62
Colwyn	53220	13572	25.50
Delyn	65431	11620	17.76
Glyndwr	40338	16076	39.85
Rhuddlan	52546	8492	16.16
Wrexham Maelor	110775	14866	13.42
Carmarthen	53318	30919	57.99
Ceredigion	60980	36026	59.08
Dinefwr	37297	24811	66.52
Llanelli	72048	33483	46.47
Preseli Pembrokeshire	67571	16454	24.35
South Pembrokeshire	40314	3305	8.20
Blaenau Gwent	72937	1696	2.33
Islwyn	63440	2183	3.44
Monmouth	73301	1458	1.99
Newport	127356	2874	2.26
Torfaen	86760	2128	2.45
Aberconwy	51184	18440	36.03
Arfon	51092	38119	74.61
Dwyfor	26246	19798	75.43
Meirionnydd	31815	20816	65.43
Ynys Môn	66525	41240	61.99

(Table 6.2 continued)

Districts	1	2	3
Cynon Valley	62409	5933	9.51
Merthyr Tydfil	56662	4237	7.48
Ogwr	127087	10544	8.30
Rhondda	75085	6123	8.15
Rhymney Valley	98936	7531	7.61
Taff–Ely	91477	8895	9.72
Brecknock	39836	9175	23.03
Montgomeryshire	50676	11796	23.28
Radnor	22823	1900	8.32
Cardiff	266758	17171	6.44
Vale of Glamorgan	109099	7370	6.76
Lliw Valley	60588	22369	36.92
Neath	63051	8177	12.97
Port Talbot	49178	4222	8.59
Swansea	174962	17500	10.00
Wales	**2723623**	**508098**	**18.65**

KEY

1. Resident population aged 3 years and over

2. Population able to speak Welsh

3. Percentage population able to speak Welsh

The proportional circles associated with wards in the rural heartlands of Dyfed and Gwynedd confirm the presence of high numbers of Welsh-speakers, but they are widely dispersed in distribution. Finally, Figure 6.1 shows that the Welsh-speaking population is particularly sparse in the uplands of central Wales, the central borderland and South Pembrokeshire.

Figure 6.2 is of interest in this regard, for it displays the density of Welsh-speakers per km^2. The distribution is based on quartiles, with the lower, middle and upper limits being 14, 51 and 168, respectively. Because of the sizes of wards in upland regions, and the low absolute numbers of speakers in much of the borderland, densities of less than 14 per km^2 are to be found over an extensive area. Wards falling into the second quartile, with densities between 14 and 51, are mainly located either in lowland rural regions of west Wales (e.g., Ynys Môn, Dwyfor and Ceredigion) or on the peripheries of the major urban areas in north and south Wales. Fifty per cent of wards have densities of Welsh-speakers in excess of 51 per km^2. By and large these include the two zones of high absolute values identified above, together with isolated urban settlements along the western coast and inland.

A general feature that emerges from Figures 6.1 and 6.2 (and one that has already been alluded to) is that in terms of absolute numbers and densities the majority of Welsh-speakers are associated with dominantly urban and sub-urban areas. Given the trends that have been identified previously, it is to be expected that the urbanization of the Welsh-speaking population is likely to continue, and at an increased pace.

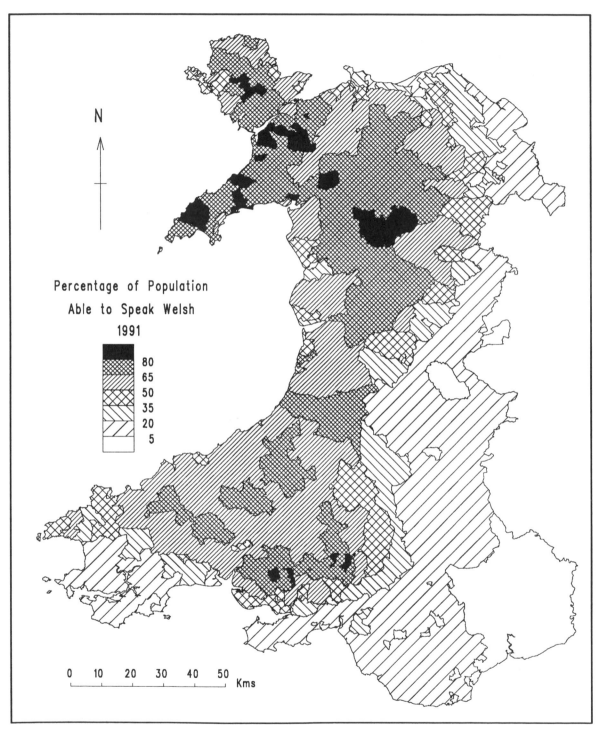

Percentage of Population
Able to Speak Welsh
1991

	80
	65
	50
	35
	20
	5

0   10   20   30   40   50   Kms

Figure 6.3

While these latter tendencies are significant, it is evident from Figure 6.3 that in terms of relative proportions, the main strongholds of the language are still to be found in rural Wales. Before commenting on these patterns in more detail it is perhaps worth reiterating that past censuses have all drawn attention to the gradual break-up of a once discrete and distinctive core area (*Y Fro Gymraeg*). Whereas the notion of a westward-moving frontier of Anglicization initially sufficed to define the encroachment on the Welsh-speaking heartland, the situation eventually became more complex as a variety of internal fracture lines established themselves.

The sequence of geolinguistic change in terms of the core area can be summarized thus:

1901   A clear and dominant core could be identified where over 90% of the population spoke Welsh.

1931   The situation was as it was in 1901, but the qualifying proportion for the core had to be reduced to 80%.

1951   The core area was still identifiable, but the qualifying threshold was nearer 75%. Internal fracture lines were becoming more and more evident.

1961   In order to justify a clear core the qualifying proportion had to be reduced yet again, this time to 65%. Four main fracture lines could be discerned :

(i)   the Menai Straits
(ii)   the Conwy–Porthmadog 'trench' across Snowdonia
(iii)   the Severn–Dyfi break
(iv)   the 'depression' between rural and industrial Dyfed

1971   The fracture lines had become so apparent that, to retain the 65% threshold, it was necessary to recast interpretation in the form of a series of separated sub-cores. They were :

(i)   Ynys Môn
(ii)   Llŷn and Arfon
(iii)   Meirionnydd–Nant Conwy
(iv)   Rural Dyfed, north of the Landsker
(v)   Industrial east Dyfed and western parts of West Glamorgan

1981   The processes which had been evident since 1951 continued apace, and the heartland was now deeply severed. The sub-cores of 1971 had become a series of peaks rising from a low ridge.

Although not on the same spatial or population bases a comparison of the patterns depicted in Figures 6.3 and 6.4 suggest that the process of change maintained its momentum between 1981 and 1991. The four rural sub-cores continued to retract and decline in strength. In north Wales, central parts of Ynys Môn, and much of Dwyfor and Arfon are still seen to be the main centres of concentration for the language, with more

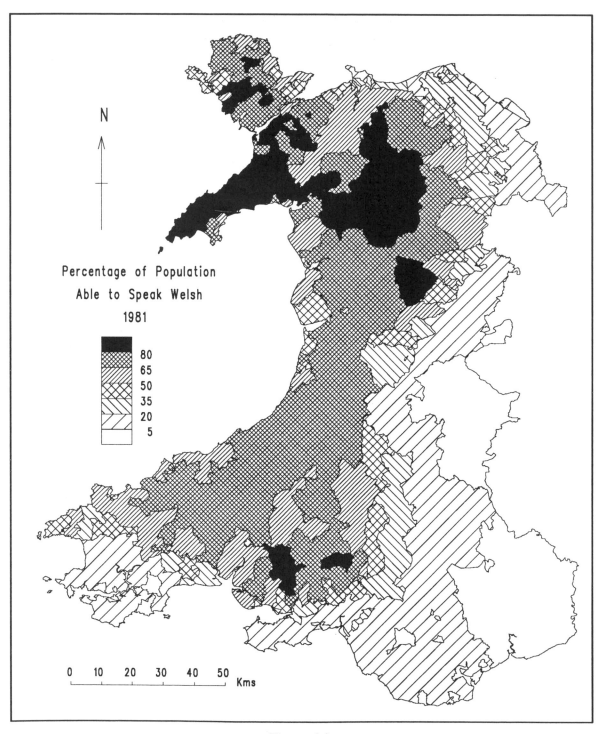

Percentage of Population
Able to Speak Welsh
1981

80
65
50
35
20
5

0 10 20 30 40 50   Kms

Figure 6.4

than 65 per cent of the population in many wards being able to speak Welsh. That said, the sub-core that centres on the uplands of Gwynedd and western Clwyd is weaker than it was, and is evidently being attenuated. Increased Anglicization of the coastal fringes and along the eastern margins is constraining this once highly-resistant bastion of the language. The process of fragmentation is most clearly manifest, however, in the uplands of rural Dyfed. In 1981 large parts of this area recorded percentages of Welsh-speakers in excess of 65; now such values apply to much reduced islands along the main rim of the Cambrian Mountains. Figure 6.4 indicates that the final, fifth, core area associated with industrial south-east Dyfed (with an extension into West Glamorgan) is still in evidence, although less sharply delineated.

Beyond the main areas of concentration the percentage of Welsh-speakers falls away rather rapidly, with gradients being at their steepest in south and central Wales. In the districts of Radnor, eastern Brecknock, Gwent, South Glamorgan and much of Mid Glamorgan less than 20 per cent of ward populations are able to speak Welsh. However, it is evident that percentages in these areas are slowly rising as the measures to promote Welsh-language teaching take effect.

Before moving on to consider other language distributions, it is worth making reference to county statistics that allow more precise specifications of rates of change in numbers of Welsh-speakers for the period 1981–91. Derived from the County Monitors and using the 1981 population base (see chapter 2), the data in Table 6.3 show that, while the overall decline in the number of Welsh-speakers was 1.4 per cent (cf. 6.3% for the previous intercensal period), changes at the county level varied greatly. The high proportionate increase in South Glamorgan (14%) was to be expected (given the developments described previously), but it did little more than compensate for the major losses (absolute and relative) in West Glamorgan (-11%), and to a lesser extent Dyfed (-2.7%). Elsewhere movements in the number of speakers were marginal, with some reductions and some advances. At the time of writing, comparable (1981 base) data had not been published for the districts of Wales.

Table 6.3
Numbers of Welsh-speakers, 1981–1991 (1981 base)

County	1981	1991	% Change
Clwyd	69578	69945	0.5
Dyfed	146213	142209	-2.7
Gwynedd	135067	135366	0.2
Mid Glamorgan	42691	42150	-1.3
Powys	21358	22355	4.7
South Glamorgan	20684	23593	14.0
West Glamorgan	57408	50976	-11.2
Wales	**503549**	**496530**	**-1.4**

Literacy

The 1991 census contains a range of information relating to language skills. Table 6.4 shows that, in all, 546,551 persons are able *either* to speak, read or write Welsh. It should be noted that this figure is significantly higher than the total number of Welsh-speakers detailed above, and suggests a stronger representation of the language. Of this total, just over two-thirds (67.6%) are fully literate and can speak, read and write the language (369,609). Although no indication is given as to the degree of proficiency on these three fronts, the figure is still very high. It is even more so if related solely to the Welsh-speaking population; in this case the percentage value increases to 72.7 per cent (cf. 72% for the 1981 census). The published statistics also indicate that a further 38,191 residents (6.9%) are able to speak and read Welsh, but not write it. Just over 100,000 people could speak, but not read or write Welsh. Nearly 37,000 maintained that they could read the language but did not speak it; a small number (1,678) even indicated that they could write but not speak Welsh. These latter statistics appear bizarre but can no doubt be partly explained as arising from variations in the interpretation of the census question 'Does the person speak Welsh?'. As has been mentioned elsewhere, this can be interpreted to mean do you 'normally' or 'habitually' speak Welsh, rather than are you able to. If this explanation is correct then it is to be expected that there will be people who, in completing the census questionnaire, legitimately claim that they do not speak the language but do read or write it. The fact that reading and/or writing can take place without social discourse is also of some relevance.

Table 6.5 specifies the proportion of Welsh-speakers within each of the counties that are (i) only able to speak Welsh, (ii) able to speak and read but not write Welsh, (iii) able to speak, read *and* write Welsh. The results are very revealing. They show that there are distinctive regional differences in patterns of literacy. Thus, it is evident that the main Welsh-speaking county of Gwynedd is characterized by a high level of literacy, with nearly 83 per cent of the Welsh-speaking population being able to read and write the language. Somewhat lower percentages apply in Dyfed (72.9%), largely because of internal regional differences in language skills (see below). Interestingly, similar proportions of the population are able to read and write Welsh in the counties of South Glamorgan (71.7%) and Clwyd (71.0%). The explanation here lies of course in the growth in the number of young Welsh-speakers who have been educated in Welsh-medium schools and, especially in South Glamorgan, the generally high socio-economic status of Welsh-speaking families. As has been demonstrated, attitudes to Welsh in these areas have changed dramatically over recent years.

Language skills are at their lowest in West Glamorgan. Here just 57.7 per cent of the Welsh-speaking population is able to read and write the language. Part of the reason for such a low rating lies in the age profiles for the area (see below). Interestingly, this county does however return the highest proportion of speakers (13.1%) who are able to speak and read Welsh (but not write it). The county of Gwent also records a high figure for the percentage of the Welsh-speaking community who are not able to read and write the language. Again, as in West Glamorgan, the age structure of the population is relevant here, but not for the same reasons.

Finally, it is worth drawing attention to the unusually high number of people in Mid Glamorgan who are apparently able to read Welsh, but who do not speak or write the language (Table 6.4).

Table 6.4
The Welsh language in 1991: literacy categories

County	1	2	3	4	5	6
Clwyd	50696	5364	15345	5779	351	77535
Dyfed	105756	11576	27666	4573	242	149813
Gwent	6326	855	3158	1492	75	11906
Gwynedd	114238	5558	18617	1981	87	140481
Mid Glam.	29373	4272	9618	11057	332	54652
Powys	15495	2014	5362	1886	98	24855
South Glam.	17582	1704	5255	3505	208	28254
West Glam.	30143	6848	15277	6502	285	59055
Wales	**369609**	**38191**	**100298**	**36775**	**1678**	**546551**

KEY

1. Able to speak, read and write Welsh
2. Able to speak and read, but not write, Welsh
3. Able to speak, but not read or write Welsh

4. Able to read, but not speak or write Welsh
5. Able to read and write, but not speak, Welsh
6. Either able to speak, read or write Welsh

Table 6.5
Literacy categories: percentage of Welsh-speaking population by county

	1	2	3
Clwyd	21.5	7.5	71.0
Dyfed	19.1	8.0	72.9
Gwent	30.6	8.2	61.2
Gwynedd	13.5	4.0	82.5
Mid Glamorgan	22.2	9.9	67.9
Powys	23.4	8.8	67.8
South Glamorgan	21.4	6.9	71.7
West Glamorgan	29.2	13.1	57.7

KEY

1. % only able to speak Welsh
2. % able to speak and read, but not write Welsh
3. % able to speak, read and write Welsh

Table 6.6 lists percentages for these three literacy categories at district level. To highlight more detailed regional patterns of variation Figure 6.5 records the proportions of the Welsh-speaking population that are able to read and write Welsh at the ward level. The

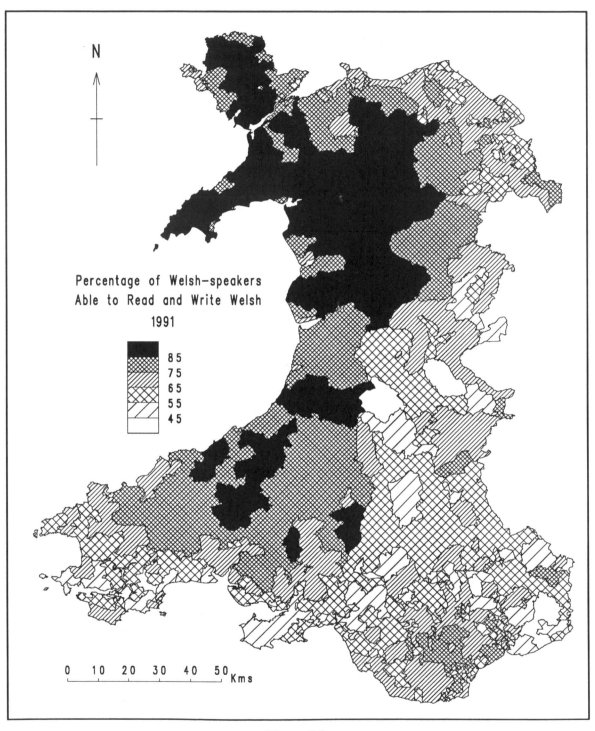

Figure 6.5

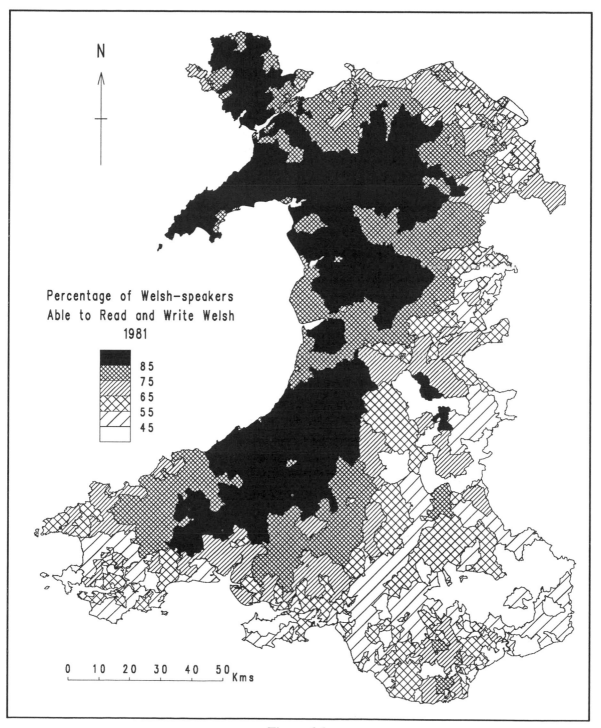

Percentage of Welsh-speakers
Able to Read and Write Welsh
1981

85
75
65
55
45

0 10 20 30 40 50
Kms

Figure 6.6

map confirms the strength of the language throughout much of Gwynedd, with literacy rates exceeding 85 per cent in many areas. Central parts of Ynys Môn, much of Dwyfor, and the central core of Meirionnydd (in association with neighbouring areas such as the Mynydd Hiraethog region of Clwyd) form a solid and very dominant cluster. Together they define what might be termed the 'articulate heartland' of the language. Similar values obtain in parts of Dyfed, but it is worth noting that the position here has changed dramatically since 1981 (Figure 6.6). The maps are not directly comparable because of boundary changes, but the reduction in the number of wards where over 85 per cent of the Welsh-speaking population are able to read and write the language is significant. In 1981 the greater part of Ceredigion and northern Carmarthen returned literacy percentages of over 85. By 1991 such areas had contracted to just three fragmented blocks. Elsewhere in Wales the figures indicate a significant increase in literacy ratios. The advance in numbers of young, and literate Welsh-speakers in many eastern and southern regions of Wales (especially in the hinterland of Cardiff) is a feature of some significance.

Table 6.6
Literacy categories: percentage of Welsh-speaking
population by district

District	1	2	3
Alyn and Deeside	24.33	6.15	69.52
Colwyn	18.49	6.01	75.49
Delyn	22.81	8.38	68.81
Glyndwr	19.02	6.66	74.33
Rhuddlan	22.83	8.02	69.15
Wrexham Maelor	23.81	9.46	66.73
Carmarthen	16.39	6.91	76.70
Ceredigion	13.60	5.04	81.36
Dinefwr	18.63	8.47	72.90
Llanelli	25.42	11.30	63.29
Preseli Pembrokeshire	21.35	8.79	69.86
South Pembrokeshire	31.83	8.93	59.24
Blaenau Gwent	35.38	6.66	57.96
Islwyn	30.74	6.41	62.85
Monmouth	28.46	12.48	59.05
Newport	29.40	8.70	61.90
Torfaen	29.46	7.99	62.55
Aberconwy	20.10	6.57	73.33
Arfon	12.89	3.76	83.35
Dwyfor	8.13	2.12	89.76
Meirionnydd	10.28	3.40	86.33
Ynys Môn	15.15	4.33	80.52
Cynon Valley	26.77	13.01	60.22
Merthyr Tydfil	26.81	12.72	60.47
Ogwr	22.93	11.24	65.83

(Table 6.6 continued)

District	1	2	3
Rhondda	22.52	11.68	65.80
Rhymney Valley	20.36	6.98	72.66
Taff–Ely	17.58	6.01	76.40
Brecknock	28.05	11.49	60.46
Montgomeryshire	19.46	6.89	73.65
Radnor	25.95	7.74	66.32
Cardiff	21.01	6.85	72.14
Vale of Glamorgan	22.36	7.15	70.49
Lliw Valley	28.17	12.54	59.29
Neath	29.31	13.55	57.14
Port Talbot	29.80	15.37	54.83
Swansea	30.40	13.06	56.54

KEY

1. *% only able to speak Welsh*
2. *% able to speak and read, but not write Welsh*
3. *% able to speak, read and write Welsh*

Age Structures

The age structure of the Welsh-speaking population has long been recognized as being of crucial importance to the survival of the language. The dangers of an age pyramid dominated by elderly speakers are obvious. It is therefore appropriate to examine age profiles for 1991 in some detail. Table 6.7 shows that 22 per cent of Welsh-speakers are under 15 years of age, as compared with 21.7 per cent for those aged over 65. The highest percentages for the 3-15 age group are seen to be associated with those counties that have experienced a growth in the number of young speakers following a significant expansion of Welsh-language education. In Gwent, Mid Glamorgan and South Glamorgan more than 30 per cent of Welsh speakers are under 15. This contrasts with the situation prevailing in West Glamorgan and Dyfed where the age group accounts for less than 20 per cent of the Welsh-speaking population. West Glamorgan is also distinguished by the very high proportion of speakers that are over 65. With such an age profile the prospects for the language in this region, at least in the short term, are not promising.

The dramatic nature of the changes currently taking place in the age structure of the Welsh-speaking population is revealed in Table 6.8. The data presented here are at the 1981 base and record numbers, percentages and percentage rates of change for Welsh-speakers under the age of 15 years. They show that between 1981 and 1991 numbers of young speakers increased by a remarkable 22.8 per cent. The advances in Gwent, Mid Glamorgan and Powys are of a particularly high order, but of course relate to relatively small numbers. Interestingly, of all the counties only Gwynedd showed a decrease (-3.1%) in its number of young Welsh-speakers. Table 6.8 also indicates that in addition to widespread gains in absolute numbers, the relative proportions of the 3–15 age group able

103

to speak Welsh also increased in all counties. Despite falling total numbers, the county of Gwynedd stands out as the main hearth area for the language; here nearly 78 per cent of the 3–15 age group are able to speak Welsh. In Dyfed, the second most important county, the figure is much lower at 47.7 per cent. Given the relatively large numbers of Welsh-speakers in the county, a figure of 15 per cent for West Glamorgan must be regarded as particularly disappointing. The scope for an expansion in the number of young Welsh-speakers in this, and the other counties of south Wales, is clearly considerable.

Table 6.7
Welsh speakers: age profiles

	Under 15		Over 65	
	Numbers	%	Numbers	%
Clwyd	18335	25.7	15187	21.3
Dyfed	26086	18.0	33820	23.3
Gwent	3558	34.4	1456	14.1
Gwynedd	28256	20.4	25974	18.7
Mid Glamorgan	14786	34.2	9801	22.7
Powys	5517	24.1	5100	22.3
South Glamorgan	7888	32.1	3028	12.3
West Glamorgan	8810	16.9	16527	31.6
Wales	**113236**	**22.3**	**110893**	**21.8**

Table 6.8
Welsh speakers: 3–15 years (1981 base)

County	1981 %	1991 %	1981* Numbers	1991* Numbers	1981–91 % Change
Clwyd	18.6	27.9	13796	18167	31.7
Dyfed	40.3	47.7	23163	25811	11.4
Gwent	2.3	4.8	1921	3490	81.1
Gwynedd	69.3	77.6	28785	27889	-3.1
Mid Glamorgan	8.6	16.1	8906	14604	64.0
Powys	16.7	30.0	3284	5463	66.4
South Glamorgan	7.4	11.9	5152	7690	49.3
West Glamorgan	9.3	15.0	6064	8719	43.8

Rounded values based on proportions in County Monitors

While the results of the 1991 census are encouraging, and have been widely publicized, they need to be treated with some circumspection. Statistics from the Committee for the Development of Welsh Education, for instance, would suggest that the situation is not as solidly based as it might be. Table 6.9 shows the percentages of children between 5 and 11 years of age who in 1988 spoke Welsh at home, who were fluent even though not speaking

Welsh at home, who spoke some Welsh, and finally who had no Welsh at all. The data are not directly comparable of course, but they do indicate that many of those returned as speaking Welsh in the census were likely to have only a rudimentary facility, and this even in the main heartland areas.

Table 6.9
Primary school children (5–11 years) by ability to speak Welsh, 1988/1989

County	1	2	3	4
Clwyd	4.3	5.9	24.0	65.8
Dyfed	19.5	9.0	22.7	48.8
Gwent	0.5	1.3	0.2	98.0
Gwynedd	39.2	19.5	32.0	9.3
Mid Glamorgan	1.0	9.0	5.5	84.3
Powys	5.5	4.2	21.3	59.0
South Glamorgan	1.3	2.6	10.6	85.5
West Glamorgan	2.8	3.3	4.1	89.8
Wales	**7.0**	**6.4**	**12.6**	**74.0**

KEY
1. *Speak at home*
2. *Fluent but do not speak at home*
3. *Speak but not fluent*
4. *No Welsh*

Source: Pwyllgor Datblygu Addysg Gymraeg, 1991

Figure 6.7 categorizes wards according to the proportion of Welsh-speakers aged between 3 and 15 years. A dominant feature of the distribution is an extensive zone where young Welsh-speakers consistently account for between 15 and 25 per cent of the Welsh-speaking population. By and large, this zone encompasses the main Welsh-speaking areas of rural Wales. Surrounding this core region is a patchwork fringe area where the proportions are generally of a higher order. Although absolute numbers are still small, the patterns draw attention to the significant impact of recent Welsh-language teaching initiatives in areas such as eastern Clwyd, the whole of Radnor, South Pembrokeshire, South Glamorgan, the Cardiff region, eastern parts of Mid Glamorgan, and western Gwent. Here the percentages of young speakers frequently exceed 35; in many wards they are even over 45.

A much more fragmented spatial pattern emerges when reference is made to the proportion of Welsh-speakers that are over 65 years of age (Figure 6.8). The greatest concentrations of older Welsh-speakers are to be found in West Glamorgan and western parts of Mid Glamorgan. A band of wards can be identified extending from the Gower Peninsula through to a zone that embraces the upland plateau and former mining valleys to the south-east of the Vale of Neath. Here more than 40 per cent of the Welsh-speaking population is over 65 years of age. A sharp and telling gradient divides this region from the more youthful Welsh-speaking areas of South Glamorgan. Throughout the main Welsh-

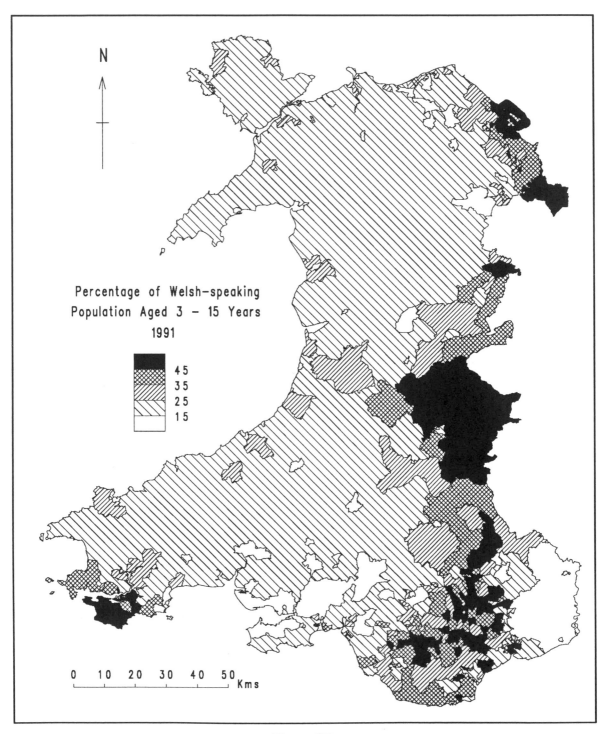

N

Percentage of Welsh-speaking
Population Aged 3 – 15 Years
1991

45
35
25
15

0   10   20   30   40   50
                        Kms

Figure 6.7

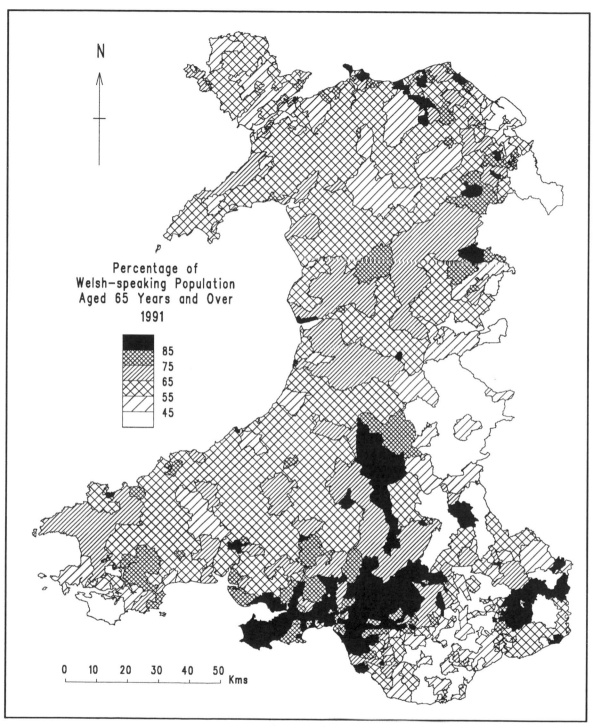

Percentage of
Welsh-speaking Population
Aged 65 Years and Over
1991

85
75
65
55
45

0   10   20   30   40   50   Kms

Figure 6.8

speaking areas of rural Wales the proportion of older Welsh-speakers varies locally, ranging generally between 15 and 25 per cent.

Finally, in exploring the geography of the language the issue of population movements is clearly of critical significance. Published statistics do not allow a precise evaluation of the impacts of such movements on the language, but some broad insights can be gained through reference to the place of birth of Welsh-speakers. In 1991, of the total resident population in Wales (2,835,073), some 77 per cent were born in Wales (Table 6.10).

Table 6.10
Place of birth by language spoken

	Resident population	
	Welsh-speaking	Non-Welsh-speaking
Born in Wales	459179	1728520
Born outside Wales	48919	598455

Figure 6.9 classifies wards according to the proportion of the resident population born in Wales. One core area dominates the picture: the old industrial and coal-mining region of south Wales. In this region percentages generally exceed 80, with a large cluster of wards actually returning values of more than 90 per cent. Percentages of between 80 and 90 apply in a scattering of wards in various parts of Wales, but for most rural areas values tend to range between 60 and 70. Only along the fringes of the borderland, in the Vale of Powys, and in regions heavily affected by in-migration (e.g., retirement areas along the coast of north Wales) is the non-Welsh-born population dominant.

In terms of the Welsh language it is of interest to note that of the total population able to speak Welsh (508,098), nearly 10 per cent (48,919) were born outside Wales (Table 6.10). This is of some significance for it demonstrates the degree to which incomers have committed themselves to learning the language. Unfortunately it is not possible to break these figures down according to age.

Welsh Office Social Survey 1992

In 1992 the Welsh Office undertook a social survey of households in Wales, and collated data relating to the language. The aim was to derive more insights into patterns of language use than is possible from the census returns. It is not necessary to enter into a detailed consideration of these very interesting results, but a few observations are in order. Firstly, the statistics were drawn from a sample of nearly 13,000 households. Secondly, the Welsh language figures are broadly in line with those derived from the 1991 census, although they tend to yield slightly higher values in terms of the incidence of Welsh-speakers. Thus, the survey suggests that 21.5 per cent of the population speak Welsh, as opposed to 18.6 per cent in the census. Thirdly, in regard to proficiency and use of the language, the survey

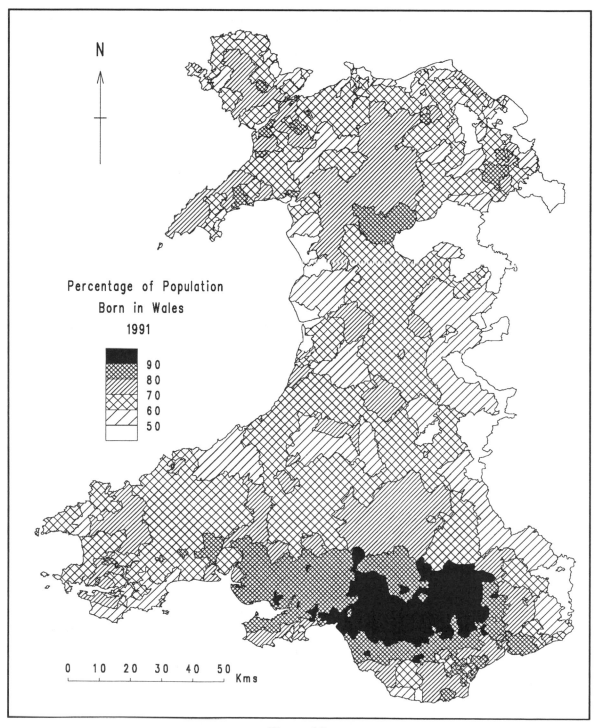

Percentage of Population
Born in Wales
1991

90
80
70
60
50

0 10 20 30 40 50 Kms

Figure 6.9

suggests that for 56 per cent of speakers (just 12% of the total population) Welsh is their mother tongue. There are, however, considerable differences between age groups. Only 27 per cent of Welsh-speakers aged between 3 and 15 have Welsh as their mother tongue, compared with 79 per cent for those over 65. This finding substantiates those made previously concerning the home backgrounds of many young Welsh-speakers (e.g., in the Cardiff region). If reference is made just to those who would regard themselves as fluent in Welsh then the proportion of Welsh-speakers stands at 13.4 per cent. Significantly, it appears that notable proportions of Welsh-speaking parents do not transmit the language fully to their children. For example, where both parents speak Welsh only 81 per cent of the children aged between 3 and 15 are fluent. Of the fluent Welsh-speakers, some 62 per cent claimed that they spoke Welsh most of the time. Inevitably the figures varied greatly from region to region, with the highest percentages being 79 and 71 in Gwynedd and Dyfed, respectively. In general, the results of this survey confirm many of the findings of the local studies described in chapter 5. They also confirm doubts raised previously concerning the true strength of the language, and the meaningfulness of any turnaround, if and when it comes.

Conclusion

It is evident from the above analyses, constrained as they are by limitations in the structure of the data and changes to the boundaries of the census areas, that many of the long-term trends predicted for the Welsh language are in the process of being realized. The pace of absolute decline in the number of Welsh-speakers has slackened considerably and the effects of thirty years of new initiatives would appear to be slowly turning the tide. The situation is not without its complications and uncertainties however. In a brief assessment of the results of the 1991 census, Aitchison and Carter (1993) set the evidence of a 'broken heartland' alongside that depicting a resurgence of commitment to the language. It was concluded that 1991 could well mark a watershed of historic consequence, but that the struggle to ensure a sustainable future for the language would have to continue.

CHAPTER 7

Towards a Golden Age?

In 1885 D. Issac Davies looked forward to a Welsh-speaking population of 3 million by 1985; less sanguine about the future, Saunders Lewis in 1962 saw the possibility of the demise of Welsh as a living language by the year 2000. The first prognostication has not been realized, the second will certainly not apply. As has been intimated, the future is brighter, but at this stage a little uncertain. Whether or not a golden age is about to be entered is still open to question, but it is certainly a possibility if the efforts of language protagonists are maintained. Unfortunately, much depends upon the cultural impress of forces that lie beyond Wales. Much has been achieved, but the sisyphean task will become that much more demanding as the summit is approached.

Predicting and monitoring the future of the language is difficult at the best of times, it is made more so by the poverty of the population census in terms of language information. The Colloquium on Minority-Language Population-Censuses and Speech-Community Surveys (European Bureau of Lesser-Used Languages) has stressed that there are serious deficiencies that need to be addressed in regards to the compilation of data for lesser-used languages. The problems concern the nature of the questions asked and the form in which they are presented. As has been demonstrated here, continued modifications to the areal boundaries of census tracts create major problems for geolinguistic studies. Compared with approaches adopted elsewhere (e.g., Canada) the situation is woefully inadequate, and needs to be accorded serious re-consideration by OPCS. Without detailed statistical information, sound language planning is impossible.

Statistical inadequacies apart, what of the future for the Welsh language? In 1991, and based on a scrutiny of movements at community level between 1961 and 1981, Aitchison and Carter opined that:

> Numbers of Welsh-speakers will continue to decline until the year 2001, but that thereafter there will be a notable reversal of the trend, with numbers increasing sharply. Whilst this scenario augers well for the language, it is based on a major reshaping of the geography of language distribution. It seems that the situation will deteriorate most rapidly in those rural communities where absolute numbers of Welsh-speakers are already rather low. Here it only takes minor movements in population for the linguistic balance to be severely disrupted. . . The predicted overall turnaround in numbers of Welsh- speakers by the year 2001 is explained by a continuance of the rapid advances recently recorded in the borderland areas of Wales, and in particular the increases that could be returned in main urban centres such as Cardiff and its immediate hinterland, Newport, Mold and

Llandrindod Wells. Such are the sizes of population in these and other centres that they could more than compensate for the small absolute losses that are likely to happen in the most vulnerable parts of rural Wales, as well as the more serious decline that could take place in those industrial regions of West Glamorgan and south-east Dyfed which currently have large numbers of Welsh-speakers.

The results of the 1991 census suggest no reason why those conclusions should be altered. But they also suggest that the standard interpretations of the geographical distribution of the Welsh language are no longer true, or at least, are becoming increasingly inappropriate. Though maintainable in a modified form, the bipolar model of an 'Inner' and an 'Outer' Wales is now much less of an imperative than it was. In the old core, to use that rather more neutral term, the language is much less dominant, especially in the relative sense which dominance implies. The proportion of Welsh-speakers which could safely be taken to define the core in 1901 was 90 per cent, in 1991 in order to define a core with equal confidence the proportion must be reduced to 50 per cent. Reductions in literacy levels in certain parts of the heartland are also indicative of a major linguistic re-structuring in Pura Wallia.

However, the decline in the heartland has a reciprocal in the resurgence that has been identified in areas lying outside it. As has been indicated, the statistics on which this trend is based need to be treated circumspectly, especially those relating to the language proficiency of young Welsh-speakers. Statistical meaningfulness apart, it is equally questionable as to whether or not these young 'green shoots' will continue to grow in what is essentially an Anglicized environment. Both those matters may well be crucial for the future of the language.

Two related issues need to be adumbrated. The first is that Welsh is now, and has been from the last century, a predominantly urban language. It is difficult to specify the level of urbanization precisely, but the general proposition is surely undeniable. For the language this urban condition poses a problem, for all towns are, by their very nature, meeting points. In a frequently quoted summary by Lewis Mumford,

> In the city remote forces and influences intermingle with the local: their conflicts are no less significant than their harmonies. And here, through the concentration of the means of intercourse in the market and the meeting place, alternative modes of living present themselves: the rutted ways of the village cease to be coercive and the ancestral goals cease to be all-sufficient: strange men and women, strange interests, and stranger gods loosen the traditional ties of blood and neighbourhood. (Mumford, 1938, 4)

Towns are cosmopolitan places where Welsh is inevitably brought face to face with English. It follows that it is much more difficult to live a life wholly in Welsh in an urban area, and the larger the town the more difficult it is, regardless of the number of Welsh-speakers. Thus, if Welsh looks to the marcher and urban areas where it can be thought of as resurgent, it looks to places where it can never be considered truly and properly dominant, that is where it is the mother tongue of a significant majority. Unfortunately, the same can be increasingly said of the traditional heartland which has been showing signs of serious attenuation. If only just over a half of the population speak Welsh then the basis for a true Welsh- language community in any meaningful sense is hardly present. It is of course true that there are areas where percentages are much higher and where Welsh-speaking communities can be found. But they are now scattered and isolated; there is no longer a *Bro Gymraeg* in the sense in which it was originally conceived.

Wales is threatened, therefore, with a situation that could well parallel that in Ireland. While there may be a widespread familiarity with the language, the true Welsh- speaking areas where Welsh is the mother tongue could be reduced, like the Irish Gaeltacht, to separated fragments clinging to the north-western shores or the remoter parts of the interior. Such are some of the implications of the geographical distribution of the language. There is an obverse side to that gloomy picture. Thus, it might be argued that the array of supportive measures that have been secured and the high level of popular commitment to the language that now exists could bring about a bilingual Wales, or at least one where the personality principle could freely operate. That, too, is an implication from the census figures, if a somewhat optimistic one. But it will be a very different Wales where the cultural associates of language will be greatly changed, for the concomitant life-styles of bilingualism will be greatly different from those of traditional Welsh Wales.

It is to be appreciated that this study has been essentially descriptive in nature, and that little attempt has been made to offer prescriptions for the future well-being of the language. Although critically important, such matters lie beyond the scope of the present analysis. That said, the patterns and processes that have been displayed and elucidated are clearly of considerable importance to an understanding of the vitality of the language nationally, and in the different regions of Wales.

It will be recalled that in the opening chapter to this text reference was made to the notion of ethno-linguistic vitality and its associated components. Since this schema has implicitly underpinned the thrust and emphasis of much of the discussion, it is appropriate by way of conclusion to reflect upon the nature and significance of the various components as they currently manifest themselves in Wales. Figure 1.3 identified three main categories of structural variables that determined the vitality of a language: status, demography and institutional support.

Status

The issue of status is central to the language debate, and has been particularly prominent over recent times. The controversies surrounding the Welsh Language Act 1993 recapitulate many that have surfaced before. The Act has been roundly criticized by many concerned with the language, and it is certainly something of a lowest common denominator aimed at avoiding contention. It establishes 'a body corporate to be known as Bwrdd Yr Iaith Gymraeg or the Welsh Language Board' with 'the function of promoting and facilitating the use of the Welsh language'. The Act states that every public body which provides services to the public in Wales or exercises statutory functions in relation to the provision by other public bodies of services to the public in Wales, shall prepare a scheme specifying the measures it proposes to take as to the use of Welsh, 'so far as is both appropriate in the circumstances and reasonably practical'. It ensures the right to use Welsh in law courts, as long as due notice is given, and dictates that all official forms and circulars should be issued in Welsh. But it ostentatiously avoids the crucial issues of the official status for Welsh in Wales, which was the key item in a private members bill introduced by Dafydd Wigley and others where the first clause was 'Both Welsh and English shall be official languages in Wales'. It also does not consider the use of Welsh by private bodies. Though a step forward, its impact is likely to be less than was hoped for by language activists.

The economic status of the language is much more difficult to measure for inevitably it must rest on subjective assessment. In this regard, Glyn Williams has consistently argued the case for the subservient and dependent condition of Welsh-speakers:

> The argument focussing on the cultural division of labour can be substantiated by looking, for example, at an area such as the county of Gwynedd where there have been profound developments of branch plant and new manufacturing industries. The most obvious feature of such developments is that if the employment decisions for both manufacturing and retail are made outside Wales, at head office, then most of the higher-level managerial or professional posts will be held by in-migrants. On the other hand, if the objective is the search for cheap labour, the proletarian labour will be local. That is, we envisage two different labour markets for different class locations. . . There is a heavy under-representation of Welsh-speakers in the top four official socio-economic groups used in the census tabulations. (Williams, G., 1986, 187)

That comment is based on conclusions drawn from special tabulations of the Welsh language data from the 1981 census. Equivalent information for 1991 is not yet available, but there is no reason to question its continuing validity. On that basis, and of the continuing existence of a cultural division of labour (Hechter, 1975), then the inferior status of the language seems to remain, as do the prejudices of the last century.

While this may be so, in the detailed questionnaire surveys undertaken by Aitchison and Carter (chapter 5), the suggestion that being able to speak Welsh offers few advantages when it comes to seeking employment was forcefully rejected by pupils and parents alike. A facility in the language, it was argued, widened job opportunities considerably. Sceptics might claim that such attitudes reflect hopes and expectations rather than the realities of the situation as far as most economic sectors are concerned. In regard to highest level posts in particular, these are often determined by international firms with little or no interest in Wales other than as an advantageous location. This stance is close to the business view, constantly reiterated, that too great an emphasis on the language will deter entrepreneurs from considering investment in Wales, especially where competition from English or

Scottish regions is involved. It is part, too, of the argument of those who have reservations in relation to the development of Welsh-language education. It is evident, therefore, that the sort of nineteenth-century detraction of the language on economic grounds, the central message of the Blue Books, is still extant. But it is by no means as powerful as it was, and there is a widespread awareness of the advantages of a knowledge of Welsh, especially in public employment. With the new Welsh Language Act this is likely to increase.

These observations on economic status inevitably impinge on the issue of the social status of the language, for there is no easy distinction to be made between the two. The extent of the association of Welsh speech with social class is not easy to ascertain, and perhaps the real measure should be with the various socio-economic groups rather than with the rudimentary social class divisions of the census. Since there is no Welsh-speaking aristocracy, it is manifest that Welsh has only an inferior status in the upper ranks of the British class system, which is totally irrelevant to Wales. Certainly it is possible to argue that the old prejudices have gone and there is even an element of social cachet in being able to speak Welsh, at least in Wales. Again, the argument remains much the same as in economic status; a cultural division of labour can be identified indicating that social divisions run on linguistic lines, but surveys suggest that the ability to speak Welsh may well carry social advantages. There is a difference of course between class as perceived status and income as a measure of socio-economic well-being. Perhaps it is simply the perceived status of Welsh speech within Wales which has risen in recent times.

A third facet of the status component is the status of the language within and outside the bounds of the area in which it is spoken. Again, many of the arguments advanced above apply. Certainly, within Wales there is much less of the denigration which was once so widespread. To speak Welsh is seen more widely as the true and only symbol of Welshness, and wholly desirable. That is a view often accepted by non-Welsh-speakers who greatly regret their inability to speak Welsh. Even those who contest such a notion do not wish to diminish the status of the language as such. Internally, within Wales, therefore, although there are dissenting voices, status seems more assured than ever. The full complexity of this particular issue was discussed in chapter 1.

The view from without, presumably from England, rather than from neighbouring Celtic countries, is even more difficult to assess, for the evidence must be largely anecdotal. That said, it is certainly difficult to identify much support for the language and all that it stands for. There is evidently some opposition, as in a recent diatribe by A. N. Wilson in the *Evening Standard*, which seeks to denigrate all things to do with Welsh. Perhaps the description by Harvey Porlock of Wilson as 'the voice of high-minded vulgarity' puts the comment into context. More often there is total incomprehension that a language other than English should be the mother tongue of native British people. It is a common experience that news readers both on television and radio rarely pronounce Welsh place-names with any degree of accuracy, carrying the arrogant implication that such a necessity is unimportant, especially in comparison with major world languages where efforts at accuracy are manifestly made. In contrast, the rise of commitment to lesser-used languages has brought support from a much wider international field, and as was suggested in chapter

5, it is likely to grow in the coming decade. Perhaps the crucial factor in all this is that during the nineteenth century Welsh population migration, largely dominated by the growth of the coalfields, was internal. There was never the massive emigration which characterized the Irish and the Scots to America for instance. Thus, many Americans are totally unaware of the existence of Wales, and can make no sense of being told that someone is Welsh. This does limit the sort of external support which other minority languages can claim. The view from outside therefore is seldom greatly supportive, ranging from denigration through condescension to ignorance, although all three are possibly aspects of the same reaction. The impact of all this on vitality is impossible to assess. Outside the in-group of the other Celtic countries and those committed to lesser-used languages, there is dominantly little awareness and hence little support.

Demography

Demographic factors, which constitute the second group of variables impacting on vitality, have been largely dealt with in the course of the book and need no extensive repetition. At present, there is no evidence that the out-migration of Welsh people will slacken. Indeed, pit closures and continued de-industrialization, are likely to lead to further job losses and population shift, especially in the linguistically crucial anthracite coalfield in the south. Again, there seems little potential for growth in rural areas as farmers struggle to remain in business. In contrast, with the recession the buying of second or holiday homes has probably diminished, and so too has the process of counter-urbanization, although both evidently continue. The main trends are, in consequence, unlikely to be reversed even if they operate with somewhat reduced vigour. But there is a further problem in that the Welsh-speaking population of the heartland is increasingly elderly, as was indicated in chapter 6. Again the census does not permit the derivation of any relationship between natality, mortality and language but there is likely to be little natural increase, and possibly a natural decrease, in the areas with the greatest percentages of Welsh-speakers. In contrast, the areas with the highest proportion of young speakers are the marcher and urban areas, those regions where in an Anglicized environment it will be most difficult for school leavers to maintain their fluency and pass it on to their children. In general, therefore, it is difficult to see demographic factors as significant contributors to the vitality of the language.

Institutional Support

The third and final component in the group of influences is that of institutional support. Two types are distinguished: formal and informal. In the formal category the general status of the language and the need for complete equality with English within Wales has already been considered. Progress on this latter front has been mixed. Other initiatives, however, have been more successful, and most especially in the domains of education and

116

the media. Developments in education have been extensive, so that from pre-school nursery to University of Wales degrees, and to postgraduate qualifications also, it is now possible to follow schemes in Welsh. There are obvious lacunae, for example in the range of degree schemes offering teaching through the medium of Welsh, but progress has been considerable over the last two decades. In effect, so widespread has been the development of Welsh-medium education at all levels, including the teaching of Welsh to adults, that no brief summary here can be adequate. As has already been noted, the inclusion of Welsh in the national curriculum is of crucial importance:

> In 1988 the Education Reform Act came into force, giving Welsh the status of a core subject in Welsh-medium schools and the status of a foundation subject in the rest of the schools of Wales. At the same time, the Secretary of State for Wales established a working party to advise . . . on suitable Attainment Targets and Programmes of Study for the Welsh language. As a result, a Statutory Instrument was published as part of the National Curriculum to be operated from the start of the 1990/1991 academic year. This gives the language an enhanced status, better than ever before in its history. (National Language Forum, 1991, 19–20)

This situation has, however, been very recently modified after the Dearing Report. Welsh will no longer be a foundation subject in non-Welsh-medium schools and will, therefore, not be compulsory after the age of 14.

But the data indicate that much more needs to be achieved on the educational front. In 1988, according to statistics published by the Committee for the Development of Welsh Education, in primary schools some 1,468 classes covering 33,174 pupils, were taught wholly or mainly through the medium of Welsh, with a further 305 classes and 5,802 pupils where there was some teaching through Welsh. These, taken together, give percentages of 16.7 and 14.7. There was no Welsh taught in 3,224 classes and to 81,199 pupils, constituting 30.4 and 30.7 per cent, respectively. The figures for secondary education were generally lower. Thus, some 10.5 per cent of pupils were taught Welsh as a first language, while another 39.2 per cent were taught it as a second language. The remainder (50.3%) received no instruction whatsoever in Welsh. In considering these figures it needs to be appreciated that the situation within secondary schools varies greatly according to year. Thus, in first forms only 17.2 per cent of pupils were taught no Welsh at all.

Of great relevance are the courses and opportunities offered to adults to learn Welsh. They are given both by public and private bodies and provision is extensive. Few can claim major difficulties in gaining access to language classes for learners. Amongst the many organizations offering courses, the National Language Centre at Nant Gwrtheyrn deserves special mention, as does CYD (Cyngor y Dysgwyr) which is funded by The Welsh Office and the Development Board for Rural Wales. But local and residential courses are widely available, and even if they are inaccessible then television and radio both provide programmes for learners.

While developments in the sphere of education have been most successful and generally welcomed, there have been movements in opposition, such as Education First which opposes Dyfed's policy of classifying schools by language status. There have also been retrogressive steps, such as The Secretary of State's abolition of The Committee for the Development of Welsh Education (Pwyllgor Datblygiad Addysg Gymraeg); but these are relatively minor problems in a field of general progress.

The second of the major institutional supports for the Welsh language has been the mass media, especially television and radio. The emergence of S4C, the Welsh fourth channel, has already been referenced, and its significance assessed. Only one further point needs to be raised and this concerns the accusation that much of the Welsh on television is 'academic' in nature, and removed from everyday language. It is argued by some that this causes many to turn to such items as news programmes in English and limit their listening and viewing in Welsh. This is a difficult and contentious issue. In all, the growth in national and local transmissions through the medium of Welsh have been of crucial import to the general vitality of the language.

The third of the formal supports to be highlighted here is the area of government services. These have been substantially developed and will be even more so following the implementation of the new Language Act. A good example of developments on this front is the stance taken by the Central Council for Education and Training in Social Work (CCETSW) which is responsible for the training of social and care workers. In 1987 CCETSW's Committee in Wales proposed that a Welsh language policy should be formulated for the Council. The policy, the work of a special sub-committee, was approved in 1989 and issued as a document *Welsh Language Policy* (CCETSW, 1990). The principles of the policy are quite clear:

> CCETSW should promote and encourage equal status for the Welsh and English languages in its work in Wales . . . A client has a basic right to choose the language of interaction with the social work agency and its workers and there is, therefore, a consequent need for social workers and care workers who can offer a professional service through the medium of Welsh in all parts of Wales. CCETSW should seek to ensure that Welsh medium education and training is available for students who wish to study and practice in Welsh, and that English medium education and training is culturally and linguistically sensitive. (CCETSW, 1990, 2)

With such standards accepted in all services throughout Wales then support would be properly effective.

The informal areas of institutional support for the language have been less effectively developed, particularly in the realms of industry and business. In more local terms most of the large supermarket chains at least make a token effort at bilingualism with notices in their stores, a trend which is growing. But the opposition to the mandatory use of Welsh by industry and business on grounds of practicality and profitability remains strong and consistent. In contrast, in cultural spheres, including religion, there is evident support.

Welsh publishing is well supported by the Welsh Books Council; the Welsh Arts Council is a supporter of all forms of artistic work and overriding all is the continued thriving status of the National Eisteddfod.

Any effort, such as this, to summarize the congeries of forces that are currently impacting on the Welsh language must inevitably be highly selective and partial. A comprehensive and integrated evaluation would require very extensive elaboration. What is certain, however, is that since the 1960s an enormous amount has been achieved in revitalizing and rejuvenating the national language of Wales. However, for those seeking to protect and promote the language, it is particularly frustrating that so many of the influences that will determine its future vitality are virtually beyond control. Continually overshadowing the massive internal efforts to turn the tide of decline are powerful world-wide trends, both economic and social, which are bound to impact upon Wales and which even a devolved government would have difficulty in offsetting. To date, few of those trends in a megalopolitan world are supportive of lesser-used languages. Be this as it may, as the century draws to a close, it is possible to discern as many positive tendencies. The end of the last century saw a supposed golden age dissolve into disinterest and disillusion; a new golden era may not be in the offing, but the prospects appear much brighter. The future of the language seems assured, but as always much will depend upon the degree to which it can continue to capture the minds and hearts of the people of Wales.

APPENDIX

Number and Percentage of Welsh-speakers by Census Ward, 1991

Ward	Welsh-speakers No.	%
CLWYD		
Alyn and Deeside		
Aston	332	9.6
Buckley Bistre East	348	10.1
Buckley Bistre West	380	8.6
Buckley Mountain	140	7.1
Buckley Pentrobin	254	7.6
Caergwrle	148	8.8
Connah's Quay Central	304	9.6
Connah's Quay Golftyn	436	10.4
Connah's Quay South	473	10.8
Connah's Quay Wepre	188	8.9
Ewloe	281	8.9
Hawarden	138	7.4
Higher and East Shotton	336	8.2
Higher Kinnerton	169	11.0
Hope	291	13.2
Llanfynydd	361	21.6
Mancot	219	7.5
North and East Broughton	138	7.0
Penyffordd	388	11.6
Queensferry	118	6.5
Saltney	318	7.4
Sealand	158	5.6
South Broughton	219	6.8
Treuddyn	494	33.0
West Shotton	168	8.8
Colwyn		
Betws yn Rhos	483	52.4
Colwyn	991	23.8
Dinarth	429	16.5
Eirias	920	27.6
Gele	990	23.8
Glyn	773	19.0
Kinmel Bay	375	8.6
Llanddulas	386	24.6
Llanfair Talhaiarn	841	56.1
Llangernyw	1017	74.8
Llansannan	943	74.1
Llysfaen	546	22.8
Mochdre	517	27.1
Pentre Mawr	1043	19.8
Rhiw	840	16.7
Rhos	642	14.7
Towyn	166	8.9
Trefnant	569	33.8

Ward	Welsh-speakers No.	%
Uwchaled	1092	77.4
Delyn		
Bagillt East	327	12.7
Bagillt West	147	12.7
Caerwys	628	28.1
Castle	221	10.2
Cilcain	382	20.7
Coleshill	406	11.4
Ffynnongroyw	576	27.5
Greenfield	329	12.8
Gronant	252	16.9
Gwernaffield	303	17.2
Gwernymynydd	392	23.8
Halkyn	946	25.6
Holywell East	475	15.4
Holywell West	526	19.1
Leeswood	324	16.2
Mold Bron Coed	279	20.6
Mold Central	364	22.2
Mold East	214	15.8
Mold North	284	18.1
Mold South	469	28.2
Mold West	185	14.1
Mostyn	443	24.3
Mynydd Isa East	354	12.2
New Brighton	394	13.7
Northop	595	14.8
Oakenholt	327	11.0
Trelawny	436	12.8
Trelawnyd and Gwaenysgor	511	31.2
Whitford	515	22.7
Glyndwr		
Ceiriog Ganol	617	36.2
Chirk North	239	10.9
Chirk South	138	8.4
Corwen	1332	58.9
Denbigh Central	772	40.5
Denbigh Lower	1930	50.3
Denbigh Upper	952	39.2
Efenechtyd	644	53.1
Gwyddelwern	530	69.6
Henllan	344	47.6
Llanarmon-yn-Ial	412	25.2
Llanbedr Dyffryn Clwyd	431	32.9
Llandegla	315	39.7
Llandrillo	723	70.6
Llandyrnog	433	35.8

Ward	Welsh-speakers No.	%
Llanfair Dyffryn Clwyd	707	54.0
Llangollen	638	20.2
Llangollen Rural	446	19.8
Llanrhaeadr-ym-Mochnant	489	51.2
Llanrhaeadr-yng-Nghinmeirch	829	62.4
Llansilin	357	43.3
Llanynys	623	60.5
Ruthin	2166	44.7
Rhuddlan		
Bodelwyddan	300	18.5
Dyserth	521	22.6
Meliden	321	16.1
Prestatyn Central	620	19.0
Prestatyn East	573	15.6
Prestatyn North	489	10.6
Prestatyn South West	391	12.9
Rhuddlan	790	22.6
Rhyl East	607	13.7
Rhyl South	583	16.7
Rhyl South East	881	14.2
Rhyl South West	620	12.4
Rhyl West	562	12.0
St Asaph East	443	26.0
St Asaph West	296	18.5
Tremeirchion	529	37.4
Wrexham Maelor		
Acton	305	9.9
Borras Park	401	14.8
Bronington	225	7.8
Brymbo	322	12.5
Bryn Cefn	165	9.6
Caia Park	374	7.1
Cefn	564	12.0
Coedpoeth	994	21.4
Esclusham	377	13.3
Garden Village	321	16.5
Gresford East and West	216	8.3
Grosvenor	252	12.8
Gwenfro	135	8.0
Gwersyllt East and South	287	7.9
Gwersyllt North	191	7.8
Gwersyllt West	243	8.9
Holt	125	6.3
Johnstown	712	23.2
Little Acton	317	13.5
Llay	346	7.4
Maesydre	288	14.5

Ward	Welsh-speakers No.	%	Ward	Welsh-speakers No.	%	Ward	Welsh-speakers No.	%
Marchwiel	162	7.8	Llanarth	820	63.4	Llangennech	2048	53.3
Marford and Hoseley	217	9.9	Llanbadarn Fawr	645	45.0	Lliedi	1880	36.9
Minera	447	19.7	Llandyfriog	1052	64.4	Llwynhendy	1522	35.4
New Broughton	274	10.1	Llandysiliogogo	935	56.3	Pembrey	1464	41.1
Offa East	816	15.0	Llandysul Town	1003	75.5	Pontyberem	2162	80.5
Offa West	376	11.5	Llanfarian	667	59.6	Swiss Valley	975	38.6
Overton	224	8.6	Llanfihangel Ystrad	1207	66.0	Trimsaran	1667	64.2
Pant	798	37.9	Llangeitho	855	60.3	Tumble	2770	78.0
Penycae	777	23.5	Llangybi	739	54.7	Tycroes	1385	64.4
Plas Madoc	238	10.9	Llanrhystyd	839	67.7	Tyisha	1275	31.3
Ponciau	1841	50.8	Llansantffraid	1282	62.4	**Preseli Pembrokeshire**		
Queensway	317	6.7	Llanwenog	1161	71.4	Brawdy	477	35.0
Rhosnesni	319	11.5	Lledrod	1308	65.6	Burton	113	8.3
Rossett	197	6.9	Melindwr	1020	58.1	Camrose	266	11.9
Ruabon	377	12.5	New Quay	453	50.6	Castle	230	12.5
Stansty	227	10.4	Penbryn	1065	54.7	Cilgerran	1102	65.0
Whitegate	153	8.0	Penparc	1338	60.8	Clydey	858	64.5
DYFED			Tirymynach	986	65.3	Crymych	1487	68.8
			Treteurig	795	60.2	Dinas Cross	967	61.4
Carmarthen			Tregaron	887	78.4	Fishguard	1197	39.3
Abergwili	1146	60.4	Troedyraur	791	63.3	Garth	497	10.9
Carmarthen Town North	2286	44.8	Ystwyth	1032	64.2	Goodwick	587	31.6
Carmarthen Town South	1689	50.1	**Dinefwr**			Hakin	252	5.2
Carmarthen Town West	1632	48.3	Ammanford	1017	70.8	Johnston	156	7.6
Cenarth	1205	63.4	Betws	1116	66.9	Letterston	793	42.5
Clynderwen	816	62.4	Brynamman	734	81.1	Llangwm	145	7.8
Cynwyl Elfed	943	59.6	Castle	446	55.9	Maenclochog	911	59.4
Gorslas	2602	78.4	Cynwyl Gaeo	814	60.1	Merlin's Bridge	210	11.7
Laugharne Township	215	17.5	Ffairfach	731	64.3	Milford Central and East	244	5.6
Llanboidy	858	53.5	Garnant	1563	77.5	Milford North and West	237	6.1
Llanddarog	1262	69.6	Glanamman	1604	77.0	Newport	651	57.0
Llanddowror	371	23.1	Llandeilo	481	58.7	Neyland East	126	7.1
Llandyfaelog	826	68.3	Llandovery	927	46.9	Neyland West	113	5.5
Llanfihangel-ar-Arth	1403	68.6	Llandybie	2377	68.8	Prendergast	272	15.7
Llangeler	2004	67.2	Llanegwad	1031	61.2	Priory	193	8.1
Llangunnor	1199	52.6	Llanfair-ar-y-Bryn	490	49.1	Rudbaxton	331	16.3
Llangyndeyrn	2062	71.9	Llanfihangel Aberbythych	929	61.5	St David's	828	43.2
Llanllwni	645	62.7	Llangadog	1109	65.8	St Dogmaels	1009	55.6
Llansteffan	1010	54.7	Llynfell	752	81.8	St Ishmael's	100	6.9
Llanybydder	1035	69.7	Manordeilo	808	55.3	Scleddau	637	46.5
Newchurch	711	62.6	Myddfai	378	60.1	Solva	857	50.9
Pencarreg	821	67.2	Myddfnych	711	62.4	The Havens	121	8.7
St Clears	1798	62.1	Pantyffynnon	793	67.3	Wiston	486	32.2
St Ishmael	680	51.7	Penygroes	1677	78.5	**South Pembrokeshire**		
Trelech	995	67.8	Pontamman	821	65.7	Amroth	68	6.1
Whitland	693	47.3	Quarter Bach	827	79.1	Begelly	120	7.1
Ceredigion			Saron	2141	68.9	Carew	74	5.9
Aberaeron	1040	71.2	Talley	519	56.3	East Williamston	101	5.3
Aberporth	1026	49.6	**Llanelli**			Hundleton	88	7.8
Aberystwyth East	583	55.7	Bigyn	1946	32.7	Lampeter Velfrey	302	23.0
Aberystwyth North	884	44.9	Burry Port	1682	39.9	Lamphey	132	8.3
Aberystwyth South	1153	40.9	Bynea	1175	43.3	Manorbier	83	4.6
Aberystwyth West	976	43.4	Cross Hands	1086	80.4	Martletwy	167	13.6
Beulah	882	60.0	Dafen	1031	37.5	Narberth Rural	130	12.4
Borth	831	43.9	Elli	1300	42.1	Narberth Urban	326	18.1
Capel Dewi	759	60.9	Felinfoel	682	33.9	Pembroke Dock Central	111	7.3
Cardigan	2707	63.9	Glanymor	1099	25.3	Pembroke Dock Llanion	185	7.5
Ceulanamaesmawr	1054	61.7	Glyn	1438	73.2	Pembroke Dock Market	121	7.1
Ciliau Aeron	973	62.4	Hendy	1621	61.6	Pembroke Dock Pennar	137	5.3
Faenor	864	50.9	Hengoed	1462	41.0	Pembroke Monkton	91	5.3
Lampeter	1410	72.6	Kidwelly	1831	59.7	Pembroke St Mary	223	7.2

Ward	Welsh-speakers No.	%	Ward	Welsh-speakers No.	%	Ward	Welsh-speakers No.	%
Pembroke St Michael	222	10.5	Priory	66	2.6	Wainfelin	94	4.5
Penally	96	7.0	Raglan	30	1.7	**GWYNEDD**		
Saundersfoot	131	5.0	Rogiet	12	1.2			
Stackpole	71	10.6	Severn	86	2.0	**Aberconwy**		
Tenby	296	6.4	Shirenewton	33	1.4	Betws-y-Coed	457	55.7
			St Arvans	23	1.6	Bro Machno	739	68.4
GWENT			St Christopher's	22	1.2	Bryn	637	51.0
			St Kingsmark	54	2.2	Bryn Rhys	509	42.3
Blaenau Gwent			St Mary's	14	.9	Caerhun	964	50.1
Abertillery	53	1.2	Thornwell	55	2.9	Capelulo	607	41.8
Badminton	68	2.2	Trellech United	37	1.6	Conwy	1345	38.4
Beaufort	101	2.6	Usk	56	2.6	Craig-y-Don	680	21.2
Blaina	65	1.5	Vauxhall	63	1.6	Crwst	1081	63.3
Brynmawr	248	4.7	West End	25	1.7	Deganwy	810	23.5
Cwm	80	2.2	Wyesham	14	.7	Eglwysbach	823	58.4
Cwmtillery	69	1.4	**Newport**			Fforddlas	350	38.9
Ebbw Vale North	107	2.3	Allt-yr-yn	255	3.1	Gogarth	674	18.9
Ebbw Vale South	93	2.2	Alway	183	2.2	Gower	808	67.2
Georgetown	96	3.0	Beechwood	167	2.2	Lafan	339	46.8
Llanelly Hill	173	4.6	Bettws	123	1.5	Marl	1007	29.7
Llanhilleth	78	1.5	Caerleon	188	2.4	Mostyn	637	18.1
Nantyglo	95	2.0	Gaer	129	1.6	Pandy	944	56.9
Rassau	107	3.1	Graig	168	3.9	Pant-yr-afon	668	37.9
Sirhowy	101	1.8	Langstone	48	1.9	Penmaenan	369	47.7
Six Bells	33	1.3	Liswerry	280	3.0	Penrhyn	754	21.4
Tredegar Central and West	145	2.4	Llanwern	91	2.7	Pensarn	899	33.3
Islwyn			Malpas	196	2.4	Trefriw	680	54.4
Abercarn	62	1.3	Marshfield	67	2.3	Tudno	945	22.1
Argoed	93	3.7	Pillgwenlly	124	2.4	Uwch Conwy	738	78.3
Blackwood	344	4.9	Ringland	90	1.0	**Arfon**		
Cefn Fforest	196	5.3	Rogerstone	214	3.0	Bethel	1578	79.0
Crosskeys	93	3.0	St Julians	149	1.8	Bontnewydd	960	85.9
Crumlin	160	2.8	Shaftesbury	82	1.6	Cadnant	1619	87.4
Newbridge	116	1.8	Stow Hill	127	2.9	Deiniol	416	44.4
Pengam	248	7.0	Tredegar Park	64	2.2	Deiniolen	1110	85.0
Penmaen	98	2.3	Victoria	132	2.2	Dewi	939	63.8
Pontllanfraith	242	3.2	**Torfaen**			Garth	344	54.1
Risca East	236	3.6	Abersychan	190	2.8	Gerlan	927	72.9
Risca West	156	3.2	Blaenavon	65	1.1	Glyder	882	56.6
Ynysddu	153	4.1	Brynwern	40	2.2	Hendre	661	56.8
Monmouth			Coed Eva	101	4.1	Hirael	774	65.8
Caerwent	43	1.9	Croesyceiliog North	52	1.5	Llanberis	1553	80.9
Caldicot Castle	61	2.6	Croesyceiliog South	57	3.0	Llandwrog	1837	77.9
Cantref	94	3.1	Cwmyniscoy	30	2.0	Llandygai	1586	66.6
Castle and Grofield	42	2.1	Fairwater	189	3.9	Llanllechid/Aber	686	66.7
Croesonen	30	2.0	Greenmeadow	149	3.2	Llanllyfni	751	74.7
Crucorney	38	2.1	Llantarnam	116	2.8	Llanrug	2055	82.8
Dewstow	24	1.7	Llanyrafon North	56	2.8	Llanwnda	1447	81.4
Goetre Fawr	63	2.8	Llanyrafon South	90	3.8	Marchog	1381	55.0
Lansdown	36	2.2	New Inn Lower	55	2.1	Menai (Bangor)	534	43.0
Larkfield	26	1.8	New Inn Upper	71	2.4	Menai (Caernarfon)	1875	84.5
Llanbadoc	24	1.9	Panteg	101	1.5	Ogwen	1675	83.5
Llanfoist Fawr	41	2.7	Pontnewydd	66	1.2	Peblig	2108	90.9
Llangybi Fawr	38	2.4	Pontnewynydd	27	1.9	Penisarwaun	921	72.4
Llanover	51	2.3	Pontypool	50	2.6	Pentir	1400	64.9
Llantilio Crossenny	22	1.4	Snatchwood	21	1.1	Penygroes	1566	89.8
Llanwenarth Ultra	58	4.0	St Cadocs and Penygarn	17	1.0	Rachub	679	84.5
Magor with Undy	76	2.0	St Dials	115	2.9	Seiont	2559	89.2
Mardy	64	2.7	Trevethin	48	1.3	Talysarn	945	76.2
Mitchel Troy	20	1.7	Two Locks	164	3.6	Waunfawr	1103	73.0
Overmonnow	23	1.3	Upper Cwmbran	155	2.7	Y Felinheli	1257	72.7
Portskewett	29	1.6						

Ward	Welsh-speakers No.	%
Dwyfor		
Aberdaron	697	79.0
Abererch	1089	84.2
Abersoch	413	52.5
Beddgelert	320	61.4
Botwnnog	722	80.1
Buan	327	71.1
Clynnog	631	74.8
Criccieth	1135	67.8
Dolbenmaen	933	72.0
Efail-newydd	635	79.6
Gest	458	52.3
Llanaelhaearn	848	83.7
Llanarmon	949	71.8
Llanbedrog	573	55.1
Llanengan	772	68.7
Llanystumdwy	564	76.7
Nefyn	1908	77.1
Pistyll	382	78.9
Porthmadog East	814	89.6
Porthmadog West	564	78.2
Pwllheli North	1585	83.2
Pwllheli South	1576	81.2
Tremadog	1186	85.7
Tudweiliog	737	84.5
Meirionydd		
Aberdovey	288	34.2
Arthog	326	33.7
Bala	1531	82.2
Barmouth	999	43.3
Bowydd and Rhiw	1659	84.1
Brithdir and Llanfachreth	493	68.8
Bryn-crug	338	60.0
Conglywal and Maenofferen	2010	84.7
Corris	767	60.3
Cynfal and Teigl	590	77.1
Dolgellau	1843	72.8
Dyffryn Ardudwy	727	49.8
Harlech	1185	64.6
Llanbedr	596	54.9
Llandderfel	1146	76.8
Llanelltyd	464	69.6
Llangelynin	526	56.5
Llanuwchllyn	749	83.4
Mawddwy	401	70.1
Penrhyndeudraeth	1799	78.2
Trawsfynydd	1177	79.0
Tywyn	1163	39.6
Ynys Môn – Isle of Anglesey		
Aberffraw	1452	60.4
Amlwch	2483	66.7
Beaumaris	732	37.2
Bodffordd	1203	80.2
Bodorgan	1087	74.2
Bryngwran	1405	78.6
Brynteg	861	47.9
Cadnant	545	53.5
Cefni	1164	82.4
Cwm Cadnant	1268	55.4
Cyngar	1255	85.8
Holyhead Town	497	47.0

Ward	Welsh-speakers No.	%
Kingsland	759	53.7
Llanbadrig	776	56.2
Llanbedrgoch	655	44.4
Llanddyfnan	963	74.6
Llaneilian	1426	64.3
Llanfaethlu	1121	70.6
Llanfair Pwllgwyngyll	2216	73.8
Llanfair-yn-Neubwll	1195	46.3
Llanfihangel Ysgeifiog	1493	78.5
Llangoed	720	58.8
Llanidan	1100	70.1
Llanmerch-y-Medd	1329	78.6
London Road	940	58.4
Maeshyfryd	996	46.7
Mechell	960	64.9
Moelfre	655	56.1
Morawelon	868	52.6
Parc a'r Mynydd	708	59.4
Pentraeth	947	55.5
Porthyfelin	1199	53.6
Rhosyr	1342	66.3
Trearddur	978	44.2
Tudur	1370	86.2
Tysilio	1270	63.1
Valley	1308	57.1
MID GLAMORGAN		
Cynon Valley		
Aberaman North	404	8.1
Aberaman South	370	7.8
Abercynon	259	4.1
Aberdare East	800	12.8
Aberdare West	1098	16.3
Cwmbach	456	9.7
Hirwaun	626	15.8
Llwydcoed	216	15.8
Mountain Ash East	161	5.7
Mountain Ash West	292	6.3
Penrhiwceiber	272	4.2
Pen-y-waun	223	6.4
Rhigos	335	19.3
Ynysybwl	423	10.1
Merthyr Tydfil		
Bedlinog	226	6.5
Cyfarthfa	686	10.7
Dowlais	649	9.3
Gurnos	284	4.7
Merthyr Vale	235	5.8
Park	316	7.8
Penydarren	320	6.1
Plymouth	317	6.2
Town	462	7.2
Treharris	446	7.8
Vaynor	284	8.8
Ogwr		
Bettws	123	4.6
Blackmill	177	6.5
Blaengarw	121	6.7
Brackla	595	7.9
Caerau	299	6.6
Cefn Cribwr	117	7.1

Ward	Welsh-speakers No.	%
Coity Higher	409	8.3
Cornelly	525	8.5
Coychurch Lower	277	10.6
Laleston	389	5.7
Llangeinor	127	8.9
Llangynwyd	333	14.4
Maesteg East	551	10.8
Maesteg West	701	11.9
Morfa	352	7.7
Nantyffyllon	331	10.0
Nant-y-Moel	124	5.4
Newcastle	434	8.3
Newcastle Higher	307	7.7
Ogmore Vale	142	4.6
Oldcastle	428	10.6
Pencoed	917	10.2
Pontycymmer	166	6.7
Porthcawl East	494	7.5
Porthcawl West	905	10.0
Pyle	434	6.9
St Bride's Major	275	8.9
St Bride's Minor	340	6.2
Ynysawdre	164	6.8
Rhondda		
Cwm Clydach	198	6.3
Cymmer	299	4.9
Ferndale	483	10.7
Llwyn-y-pia	139	5.8
Maerdy	352	8.8
Pentre	442	8.5
Pen-y-graig	335	5.9
Porth	503	8.4
Tonypandy	193	5.6
Trealaw	217	5.3
Treherbert	762	11.7
Treorchy	1048	13.8
Tylorstown	401	6.0
Ynyshir	271	7.6
Ystrad	463	7.5
Rhymney Valley		
Aberbargoed	200	5.4
Abertysswg	69	4.9
Aber Valley	725	11.3
Bargoed	461	7.0
Bedwas and Trethomas	390	6.5
Darran Valley	184	7.1
Gilfach	133	6.2
Hengoed	233	5.0
Llanbradach	309	6.9
Machen	278	7.2
Maesycwmmer	177	7.8
Morgan Jones	504	8.7
Moriah	242	7.7
Nelson	356	8.8
New Tredegar	112	2.9
Penyrheol	852	8.7
Pontlottyn	73	3.8
St Cattwg	558	8.3
St James	478	7.5
St Martins	612	10.4
Tir-Phil	53	4.1

Ward	Welsh-speakers No.	%
Twyn Carno	238	9.1
Ystrad Mynach	299	8.4
Taff-Ely		
Beddau	251	8.1
Brynna	357	10.9
Church Village	281	10.0
Cilfynydd	243	9.2
Creigiau	420	15.9
Gilfach Goch	184	5.4
Glyncoch	202	6.7
Graig	145	6.4
Hawthorn	133	6.3
Ilan	174	9.8
Llanharan	245	8.9
Llanharry	175	7.8
Llantrisant Town	552	14.3
Llantwit Fardre	577	11.4
Pentyrch	489	14.2
Pont-y-Clun	464	11.1
Pontypridd Town	483	16.3
Rhondda	291	6.8
Rhydfelen Central	290	10.7
Rhydfelen Lower	116	7.5
Taffs Well	407	12.1
Talbot Green	214	9.1
Ton-teg	588	12.2
Tonyrefail East	469	7.9
Tonyrefail West	313	7.3
Trallwng	339	9.3
Treforest	230	6.8
Tyn-y-nant	271	7.5
POWYS		
Brecknock		
Aber-Craf	808	56.4
Bronllys	55	7.5
Builth	195	9.8
Bwlch	63	7.2
Crickhowell	201	9.6
Cwm-twrch	1249	65.7
Erwood	58	8.5
Felin-fâch	115	10.3
Gwernyfed	108	8.1
Hay	71	5.3
Llanafanfawr	90	8.8
Llanfrynach	109	10.2
Llangamarch	186	20.3
Llangattock	63	6.0
Llangors	94	9.1
Llangynidr	89	9.3
Llanwrtyd Wells	194	30.7
Llywel	279	40.7
Maescar	283	32.0
St David Within	157	11.4
St John	454	14.3
St Mary	289	10.8
Talgarth	148	8.4
Talybont-on-Usk	70	10.7
Tawe-Uchaf	625	41.0
The Vale of Grwyney	46	5.7
Ynyscedwyn	1235	60.3

Ward	Welsh-speakers No.	%
Yscir	172	19.4
Ystradfellte	153	26.8
Ystradgynlais	1557	59.9
Montgomeryshire		
Banwy	531	66.9
Berriew	112	8.9
Cadfarch	494	69.7
Caersws	314	22.1
Carno	323	56.8
Churchstoke	60	4.6
Dolforwyn	170	12.8
Forden	103	9.4
Glantwymyn	780	71.2
Guilsfield Within	138	14.0
Guilsfield Without	135	15.2
Kerry	127	8.0
Llanbrynmair	569	68.3
Llandinam	107	12.9
Llandrinio	147	9.7
Llandysilio	82	8.5
Llanfair Caereinion	587	41.0
Llanfihangel	513	57.9
Llanfyllin	486	39.6
Llangurig	151	23.4
Llanidloes East	330	16.7
Llanidloes West	139	24.9
Llansantffraid	290	19.2
Llanwddyn	779	60.2
Machynlleth No.1	542	60.3
Machynlleth No.2	643	60.4
Meifod	221	21.0
Mochdre	126	14.7
Montgomery	74	7.1
Newtown Central	420	14.5
Newtown East	245	12.9
Newtown Llanllwchaiarn North	268	15.6
Newtown Llanllwchaiarn West	276	16.8
Newtown South	198	10.5
Rhiewcynon	251	20.5
Trefeglwys	465	36.4
Trewern	79	9.0
Welshpool Castle	142	9.6
Welshpool Gungrog	199	9.3
Welshpool Llanerchyddol	198	9.8
Radnor		
Beguildy	47	6.9
Clyro	48	7.9
Disserth and Trecoed	82	8.2
Gladestry	50	12.0
Glasbury	76	9.4
Glascwm	55	7.8
Knighton	195	7.1
Llanbadarn Fawr	62	6.9
Llanbister	27	4.3
Llandrindod East	50	7.6
Llandrindod North	201	11.3
Llandrindod South No.1	49	7.9
Llandrindod South No.2	134	12.4
Llandrindod West	88	13.7
Llanelwedd	21	4.3
Llanfihangel Rhydithon	44	8.7

Ward	Welsh-speakers No.	%
Llangunllo	54	8.8
Llansantffraed-Cwmdeuddwr	53	12.1
Llanyre	82	7.9
Nantmel	43	7.4
New Radnor	44	10.5
Old Radnor	53	7.3
Painscastle	26	5.9
Presteigne	115	5.5
Rhayader Town	169	10.8
St Harmon	47	6.8
SOUTH GLAMORGAN		
Cardiff		
Adamsdown	309	4.5
Butetown	111	3.2
Caerau	411	4.2
Canton	1030	8.0
Cathays	615	6.5
Cyncoed	933	9.2
Ely	601	4.1
Fairwater	580	4.7
Gabalfa	341	6.4
Grangetown	408	3.5
Heath	979	8.9
Lisvane and St Mellons	373	6.3
Llandaff	989	11.9
Llandaff North	410	5.3
Llanishen	908	6.8
Llanrumney	322	2.7
Pentwyn	735	4.6
Plasnewydd	973	7.2
Radyr and St Fagans	572	11.7
Rhiwbina	1199	10.9
Riverside	973	8.4
Roath	918	9.1
Rumney	301	3.5
Splott	306	3.0
Trowbridge	430	3.6
Whitchurch and Tongwynlais	1435	10.1
Vale of Glamorgan		
Alexandra	722	6.7
Baruc	514	9.7
Buttrills	311	5.7
Cadoc	363	5.0
Castel and	134	3.6
Cornerswell	299	5.7
Court	267	5.4
Cowbridge	593	9.8
Dinas Powys	672	7.4
Dyfan	316	6.3
Gibbonsdown	226	4.2
Illtyd	538	7.5
Llandough	119	6.2
Llandow	206	11.3
Llantwit Major	595	6.3
Peterston-super-Ely	204	7.9
Rhoose	314	7.4
St Athan	219	5.9
Stanwell	260	6.9
Sully	294	7.2
Wenvoe	233	10.4

Ward	Welsh-speakers No.	%	Ward	Welsh-speakers No.	%
			Sandfields East	329	5.5
WEST GLAMORGAN			Sandfields West	364	5.4
			Tai Bach	312	6.6
Lliw Valley			**Swansea**		
Allt-Wen	891	40.1	Bishopston	391	8.3
Clydach	897	32.5	Bonymaen	607	8.6
Cwmllynfell	877	76.9	Castle	720	6.6
Dulais East	615	42.2	Cockett	1500	12.2
Godre'r graig	681	46.3	Cwmbwrla	597	7.6
Gorseinon Central	397	26.6	Dunvant	390	8.2
Gorseinon East	320	22.9	Killay	358	8.8
Gowerton East	320	16.3	Landore	450	7.1
Gowerton West	266	14.6	Llansamlet	1540	15.0
Graigfelen	361	20.5	Mayals	324	12.5
Gwaun-Cae-Gurwen	2204	79.1	Morriston	2755	17.2
Kingsbridge	1012	25.3	Mynyddbach	1093	11.3
Llangyfelach	754	25.2	Newton	332	9.6
Lower Brynamman	1044	76.6	North Gower	1160	18.4
Lower Loughor	497	23.1	Oystermouth	386	9.5
Mawr	983	53.5	Penderry	679	5.8
Penllergaer	468	21.1	Pennard	219	7.9
Penyrheol	1130	22.1	Sketty	1428	11.2
Pontardawe	2093	42.2	South Gower	184	8.3
Pontardulais	733	46.4	St Thomas	228	3.4
Rhos	744	31.4	Townhill	366	3.8
Tal-y-bont	999	51.3	Uplands	1298	10.8
Trebanos	668	47.2	West Cross	512	7.8
Upper Loughor	731	26.3			
Vardre	590	24.3			
Ystalyfera	2110	66.7			
Neath					
Aberdulais	234	11.9			
Blaengwrach	307	15.1			
Briton Ferry East	199	6.6			
Briton Ferry West	126	4.1			
Bryn-côch North	402	16.6			
Bryn-côch South	439	12.6			
Cadoxton	192	13.9			
Cimla	380	8.9			
Coedffranc Central	471	12.0			
Coedffranc North	273	12.1			
Coedffranc West	250	12.5			
Crynant	694	33.9			
Dyffryn	338	11.5			
Glynneath	893	24.3			
Neath East	346	5.8			
Neath North	411	10.3			
Neath South	345	7.5			
Onllwyn	328	25.8			
Pelenna	342	26.9			
Resolven	400	12.4			
Seven Sisters	621	27.6			
Tonna	237	11.5			
Port Talbot					
Aberavon	295	5.1			
Baglan	560	8.2			
Bryn and Cwmavon	1376	22.8			
Cymmer	163	5.1			
Glyncorrwg	75	6.1			
Gwynfi	108	6.5			
Margam	139	8.5			
Port Talbot	501	9.3			

References

Aitchison, J. W., J. Baptiste and W. J. Edwards, (1990) *Dyfed Communities: An Analysis of Electoral Registers 1970–1990*, Rural Surveys Research Unit, Department of Geography, University College of Wales, Aberystwyth (mimeo).

Aitchison, J. W. and H. Carter, (1985) *The Welsh Language: An Interpretative Atlas: 1961–1981*. Cardiff: University of Wales Press.

Aitchison, J. W. and H. Carter, (1987) *The Welsh Language in Cardiff: a quiet revolution.* Transactions of the Institute of British Geographers, new series, 12, 482–92.

Aitchison, J. W. and H. Carter, (1988) *The Welsh Language in the Cardiff Region*, Rural Surveys Research Unit, Monograph 1, Department of Geography, University College of Wales, Aberystwyth.

Aitchison, J. W. and H. Carter, (1991) 'Rural Wales and The Welsh Language' in *Rural History*, 2, 59–76.

Aitchison, J. W. and H. Carter, (1993) 'The Welsh language in 1991 – a broken heartland and a new beginning?' *Planet*, 97, 3–10.

Aitchison, J. W., H. Carter and D. Rogers, (1989) *In-migration and the Welsh Language: A Case Study of Tregaron and its Region*, Rural Surveys Research Unit, Monograph 3, Department of Geography, University College of Wales, Aberystwyth.

Baker, C. (1985) *Aspects of Bilingualism in Wales*. Clevedon: Multilingual Matters.

Beard, C. and C. Cerf, (1992) *The Official Politically Correct Dictionary and Handbook*. London: Graffion.

Bowen, E. G. (1959) *Le Pays De Galles*. Trans. Inst. Br. Geogr. 26, 1–24.

Bowen, E. G. (1964) *Daearyddiaeth Cymru fel cefndir i'w Hanes*. London: BBC.

Bowen, E. G. and H. Carter, (1975) 'Some preliminary observations on the distribution of the Welsh Language at the 1971 census'. *Geographical Journal*, 140, 432–43.

Bowen, I. (1908) *The Statutes of Wales*. London: T. Fisher Unwin.

Carter, H. (1976) 'Y Fro Gymraeg and the 1975 referendum on Sunday closing of public houses in Wales'. *Cambria*, 3, 89–101.

Carter, H. (1988) *Culture, Language and Territory*. London: BBC.

Carter, H. (1989) *Whose City? A View from the Periphery*. Trans. Inst. Br. Geogr. 14, 4–23.

Carter, H. (1992) *Yr Iaith Gymraeg mewn Oes Ôl-Fodern*. Cardiff: University of Wales – Darlith Eisteddfod y Brifysgol.

Carter, H. and J. W. Aitchison, (1986) 'Language Areas and Language Change in Wales: 1961–1981'. In *The Welsh and Their Country*, ed. I. Hume and W. T. R. Pryce, Llandysul: Gwasg Gomer for the Open University.

Carter, H. and J. G. Thomas, (1969) 'The Referendum on the Sunday opening of licensed premises in Wales as a criterion of a culture region'. *Regional Studies*, 3, 61–71.

Carter, H. and S. Williams, (1978) 'Aggregate Studies of language and Culture Change in Wales', in G. Williams, (ed.) *Social and Cultural Change in Contemporary Wales*, London: Routledge and Kegan Paul, 143–65.

Central Advisory Council for Education (Wales) (1953) The Place of Welsh and English in the *Schools of Wales*. London: HMSO.

Central Council for Education and Training in Social Work (1990) *Welsh Language Policy*. Bristol: CCETSW

Champion, A. G. (1987) *Population Deconcentration in Britain*. Seminar Papers No 49 – Geography Dept., University of Newcastle Upon Tyne, 49.

Council for The Welsh Language (1978) *A Future for The Welsh Language*. Cardiff: HMSO.

Dafis, L. (1992) *Lesser Used Languages – Assimilating Newcomers*. Carmarthen: Joint Working Party on Bilingualism in Dyfed.

Davies, J. (1990) *Hanes Cymru*. London: Penguin.

Davies, R. R. (1991) *The Age of Conquest. Wales 1063–1415*. Oxford: Oxford University Press.

Davies, W. (1982) *Wales in the Middle Ages*. Leicester: Leicester University Press.

Dofny, J. and A. Akiwowo (1980) *National and Ethnic Movements*. Beverly Hills: Sage Publications.

Edwards, H. T. (1987) 'Y Gymraeg yn y bedweredd ganrif ar bymtheg'. In G. H. Jenkins (ed.), *Cof Cenedl* 2, 119–52. Llandysul: Gwasg Gomer.

Evans, N. (1989) *National Identity in the British Isles*. Harlech: Coleg Harlech Occasional Papers in Welsh Studies No 3.

Francaviglia, R. V. (1970) 'The Mormon Landscape: Definition of an image in the American West', *Proceedings of Association of American Geographers*, 51–61.

Garrett, P., H. Giles and N. Coupland, (1989) 'The Contexts of Language Learning, Extending the Intergroup Model of Second Language acquisition'. In *Language, Communication and Culture*, ed. S. Ting-Tooney and F. Korzenny, 201–21.

Gellner, E. (1983) *Nations and Nationalism*. Oxford: Blackwell.

Giggs, J. and C. Pattie, (1991) *Croeso i Gymru. Welcome to Wales. But Welcome to whose Wales?* Working Paper 10. Dept. of Geography, University of Nottingham.

Giggs, J. and C. Pattie, (1992a) 'Croeso i Gymru – Welcome to Wales: But Welcome to Whose Wales?' *Area*, 24, 268–82.

Giggs, J. and C. Pattie, (1992b) 'Wales as a Plural Society'. *Contemporary Wales*, 5, 25–64.

Giles, H. (1977) *Language, Ethnicity and Intergroup Relations*. London: Academic Press.

Giles, H., R. Y. Bourhis, and D. M. Taylor, (1977) 'Towards a Theory of Language in Ethnic Group Relations.' In *Language, Ethnicity and Intergroup Relations*, ed. H. Giles. London: Academic Press.

Gottman, J. (1987) *Megalopolis Revisited: 25 Years Later*. Maryland: Institute of Urban Studies, University of Maryland.

Gudykunst, W. B. (1989) 'Cultural Variability in Ethnolinguistic Identity'. In *Language Communication and Culture*, ed. S. Ting-Tooney, and F. Korzenny, 222–43.

Harrison, G. J. (1978) Summary Report of a study of 'Bilingual Welsh/English Mothers in

Wales, with special regard to those rearing monolingual (English) children'. In *A Future For The Welsh Language, Council for the Welsh Language*. Appendix 3, 67–72. Cardiff: HMSO.

Harris, M. (1968) *The Rise of Anthropological Theory*. London: Routledge and Kegan Paul.

Hechter, M. (1975) *Internal Colonisation: The Celtic Fringe in British National Development, 1536–1966*. London: Routledge and Kegan Paul.

Hindley, R. (1990) *The Death of the Irish Language*. London: Routledge.

HMSO (1927) *Welsh in Education and Life*. London.

HMSO (1964) *Depopulation in Mid-Wales*. London.

HMSO (1965) *Report on the Legal Status of the Welsh Language*. London.

Hume, I. and W. T. R. Pryce, (1986) *The Welsh and Their Country*. Llandysul: Gwasg Gomer for the Open University.

Jackson, P. (1989) *Maps of Meaning*, London: Unwin Hyman.

Jenkins, G. H. (1978) *Literature, Religion and Society in Wales, 1660–1730*. Cardiff: University of Wales Press.

Jones, D. G. (1973) 'The Welsh Language Movement', in M. Stephens (ed.) *The Welsh Language Today*. Llandysul: Gwasg Gomer.

Jones, Elin. (1992) 'Economic Change and the Survival of a Minority Language: A Case Study of The Welsh Language'. In *Lesser Used Languages – Assimilating Newcomers*, ed. L. Dafis, 120–33. Carmarthen: Joint Working Party on Bilingualism in Dyfed.

Jones, E. and I. L. Griffiths, (1963) 'A Linguistic Map of Wales: 1961'. *Geographical Journal*, 129, 192–6.

Jones, I. G. (1992) *Mid Victorian Wales. The Observers and the Observed*. Cardiff: University of Wales Press.

Jones, P. N. (1976) 'Baptist Chapels as an index of cultural transition in the South Wales coalfields before 1914'. *Journal of Historical Geography*, 2, 347–60.

Lewis, R. (1973) 'The Welsh Language and The Law'. In *The Welsh Language Today*, ed. M. Stephens, 195–210. Llandysul: Gwasg Gomer.

Lewis, S. (1962) *Tynged yr Iaith*. London: BBC Publications.

Lewis, S. (1973) 'The Fate of the Language'. In *Presenting Saunders Lewis*, ed. A. R. Jones, and G. Thomas 127–41. Cardiff: University of Wales Press.

Mackey, W. F. (1988) 'Geolinguistics: Its Scope and Principles'. In *Language in Geographic Context*, ed. C. H. Williams, 20–46. Clevedon: Multilingual Matters Ltd.

Mandelbaum, D. G. (1949) *Selected Writings of Edward Sapir*. Berkley, California: University of California Press.

Meinig, D. W. (1965) 'The Mormon Culture Region: Strategies and patterns in the geography of the American West: 1847–1964'. *Annals Assoc. American Geographers*, 55, 191–220.

Morgan, K. O. (1981) *Rebirth of a Nation. Wales 1880-1980*. Oxford: Clarendon Press/University of Wales Press.

Morgan, P. (1981) *The Eighteenth Century Renaissance*. Llandybïe: Christopher Davies.

Morris, D. (1992) 'The Effect of Economic Changes on Gwynedd Society'. In *Lesser Used Languages - Assimilating Newcomers*, ed. L. Dafis, 134–57. Carmarthen: Joint Working Party on Bilingualism in Dyfed.

Mumford, L. (1938) *The Culture of Cities*. London: Secker and Warburg.

REFERENCES

National Language Forum (1991) *Language Strategy 1991–2001*. Caernarfon: National Language Forum.

Osmond, J. (1989) 'The Modernisation of Wales'. In N. Evans (ed.) *National Identity in the British Isles*. Harlech: Coleg Harlech Occasional Papers in Welsh Studies, No.3, 73–90.

Pei, M. (1971) *Invitation to Linguistics*. Southbend, Indiana: Gateway Editions.

Pryce, W. T. R. (1971) 'Parish Registers and Visitation Returns as primary sources for the population geography of the eighteenth century'. *Transactions of the Honourable Society of Cymmrodorion*, 271–93.

Pryce, W. T. R. (1978a) 'Wales as a Culture Region: Patterns of Change 1750–1971'. *Trans. Hon. Soc. Cymmrodorion* 229–61.

Pryce, W. T. R. (1978b) 'Welsh and English in Wales: A spatial analysis based on the linguistic affiliations of parochial communities'. *Bulletin of the Board of Celtic Studies*, 28, 1–36.

Pryce, W. T. R. and C. H. Williams, (1988) 'Sources and Methods in the Study of Language Areas: A Case Study of Wales'. In *Language in Geographic Context*, ed. C. H. Williams, 167–237.

Rawkins, P. H. (1979) *The Implementation of Language Policy in the Schools of Wales*. Glasgow: University of Strathclyde, Centre for the Study of Public Policy.

Rees, A. D. (1973) 'The Welsh Language in Broadcasting'. In *The Welsh Language Today*, ed. M. Stephens, 174–94. Llandysul: Gwasg Gomer.

Rees, I. B. (1973) 'The Welsh Language in Government'. In *The Welsh Language Today*, ed. M. Stephens, 211–30. Llandysul: Gwasg Gomer.

Rees, W. H. (1947) 'The Vicissitudes of the Welsh Language in the Marches of Wales'. Unpublished Ph.D., University of Wales.

Smith, A. D. (1986) *The Ethnic Origins of Nations*. Oxford: Blackwell.

Smith, L. B. (1986) 'Pwnc yr Iaith yng Nghymru 1282–1536' in G. H. Jenkins, (ed.) *Cof Cenedl*, 1—34.

Smith, P. (1975) *Houses of the Welsh Countryside. A Study in Historical Geography*. London: HMSO

Southall, J. E. (1895) *The Welsh Language Census of 1891*. Newport.

Steinfatt, T. M. (1989) 'Linguistic Relativity. Towards a Broader View'. In *Language, Communication and Culture*, ed. S. Ting-Tooney and F. Korzenny, 33–75.

Stephens, M. (1973) *The Welsh Language Today*. Llandysul: Gwasg Gomer.

The Council for Wales and Monmouthshire (1963) *Report on the Welsh Language Today*. London: HMSO.

The Welsh Language Board (1989) *The Welsh Language: A Strategy for the Future*. Cardiff: The Welsh Language Board.

Thomas, B. (1987) 'A Cauldron, A Rebirth. Population and the Welsh Language in the Nineteenth Century', *Welsh History Review*, 13, 418–37.

Thomas, Dafydd Elis. (1988) 'Ridding Wales of a Seige Mentality', *Western Mail*, 9 July 1988.

Thomas, J. G. (1956) 'The Geographical Distribution of the Welsh Language'. *Geog. Journal*, 122, 71–9.

Thomas, J. G. (1975) 'The Welsh Language'. In *Wales, A Physical, Historical and Regional Geography*, ed. E. G. Bowen, 247–63. London: Methuen.

REFERENCES

Thomas, Ned. (1988) 'Can Plaid Cymru survive until 1994?', *Planet*, 70.

S. Ting-Tooney, and F. Korzenny, (1989) *Language, Communication and Culture*. Newbury Park, California: Sage Publications. International and Introcultural Communications Annual Vol XIII.

Tudur, G. (1989) *Wyt Ti'n Cofio? Chwarter Canrif o Frwydr yr Iaith*. Talybont: Y Lolfa.

Welsh Office (1981) *Welsh in Schools*: Statement by the Secretary of State.

Williams, C. H. (1982) *National Separatism*. Cardiff: University of Wales Press.

Williams, C. H. (1984) *On Measurement and Application in Geolinguistics*. Discussion Papers in Geolinguistics, No 8, Dept. of Geography & Recreation, Stoke on Trent.

Williams, C. H. (1988) 'An Introduction to Geolinguistics'. In *Language in Geographic Context*, ed. C. H. Williams, 1–19.

Williams, C. H. (1988) *Language in Geographic Context*. Clevedon and Philadelphia: Multilingual Matters.

Williams, C. H. (1991) *Linguistic Minorities, Society and Territory*. Clevedon: Multilingual Matters.

Williams, D. (1950) *A History of Modern Wales*. London: John Murray.

Williams, D. T. (1937) 'A Linguistic Map of Wales'. *Geog. Journal*, 89, 146–51.

Williams, E. W. (1989) 'The Dynamic of Welsh Identity' in N. Evans ed. *National Identity in the British Isles*. Harlech: Coleg Harlech Occasional Papers in Welsh Studies, 3, 46–59.

Williams, G. (1979) *Religion, Language and Nationality in Wales*. Cardiff: Universty of Wales Press.

Williams, G. (1986) 'Recent Trends in The Sociology of Wales'. In *The Welsh and Their Country*, ed. I. Hume and W. T. R. Pryce, Llandysul: Gwasg Gomer.

Williams, G. (1992) *Sociolinguistics: A Sociological Antique*. London: Routledge.

Williams, Gwyn A. (1979) *When Was Wales?* London: BBC.

Williams, G. A. (1966) 'The Merthyr of Dic Penderyn'. In *Merthyr Politics: The Making of a Working Class Tradition*, ed. G. Williams, Cardiff: University of Wales Press.

Williams, J. (1985) *Digest of Welsh Historical Statistics* (2 vols.). Aberystwyth: Dept. of Economic and Social History, University College, Aberystwyth.

Williams, Jac. L. (1973) 'The Welsh Language in Education'. In *The Welsh Language Today*, ed. M. Stephens, 92–109. Llandysul: Gwasg Gomer.

Williams, S. R. (1992) *Oes y Byd i'r Iaith Gymraeg. Y Gymraeg yn ardal ddiwydiannol Sir Fynwy yn y bedwaredd ganrif ar bymtheg*. Cardiff: University of Wales Press.

Wuthnow, R. et al. (1984) *Cultural Analysis*. Boston: Routledge and Kegan Paul.

Zelinsky, W. (1973) *The Cultural Geography of The United States*. Englewood Cliffs, N. J.: Prentice-Hall Inc.